I0155188

Grace

What is It?

Copyright © 2019 by Summer McClellan
   All rights reserved. No part of this book may reproduced or transmitted in any form or by any means without written permission from the author.

ISBN---978-1-950252-03-9

"Scripture taken from the New King James Version. Copyright © 1982 by Thomas Nelson, Inc.

Grace

What Is It?

By Summer McClellan

To *Joy Belle*

Other Books by Summer McClellan

The Impossible Marriage
Faith, What is It?
Jesus is Our Example
Passing the Tests of Life

Table of Contents

Introduction

A Life of Grace

I cried all the way home from work the other day. Not because I was sad. I guess you could say they were tears of gratitude, or even amazement. Something has been stirring in me lately. I haven't been sleeping well, because of the stirring.

Well, first there is the usual stirring when I try to go to sleep at night, all the unpaid bills which I am wondering how to pay, mostly medical bills. The floor in the bathroom still needs replaced and the list of repairs is growing. Then the two recent setbacks two large car repair bills. I can't figure out where to come up with the money. But so, what, that kind of stuff has always been around.

Also, I feel like I am on a treadmill that never stops turning. I work 40+ hours a week at my job with no vacation in sight and then I babysit my three grandchildren 40+ hours a week while I am not working so their mother can work. Not to mention housework, laundry shopping etc., that never seems to end. All of this also creates a constant stir in me.

And there is yet another constant deeper stir, I want more of God, I want to be closer to God, I need more of God, I want Him, I want Him, I want Him!!!!! {Doesn't He see how busy I am? I want Him though. I need Him to just appear and spend time with me!}

But there is a new stirring. I had just started sleeping better and now I'm not sleeping again. I have been wondering if maybe our life is over, my husband and mine. I have had health problems the last few years, six surgeries, and still more health problems lately. My body has been having trouble keeping up with the pace. I can't just work a bunch of overtime when my finances get down, like I used to, I can't do it anymore. My husband Jim has health problems too, chronic depression, diabetes and COPD. He has been coughing in the night and that scares me. I don't want too ever be without him. I had always thought God was going to use us someday, but I wondered if maybe I was wrong. I even asked Him one time, "Aren't you ever going to use me?"

"Yes," He answered, "in the last move."

I am 55 and wondering if I will even make it to 70. Jim, my husband, is 65 and he has had a hard life with many addictions. Will his health make it? Is our life over? It almost seems like it. I have never gotten used by God yet. Will I miss what God had for me to do? So, I have started praying this prayer, *Lord, give us grace to finish our course in life. Unless you intervene, I don't think we will make it. Please help us do what we were created to do, help us finish by Your grace.*

So, in the middle of the night, while I wasn't sleeping, I read my own book again, *The Impossible Marriage.* It is the story of my husband, Jim and I, Summer.

We did not even have a chance in life. Jim was in trouble, it seemed like, from the second he was born. He had been incarcerated most of his life when I met him. He was being paroled for a second time on a three to fifteen-year sentence for armed robbery. He did not stay out long. His childhood and life up to that point had left him in turmoil and

2

trouble just followed him around.

Not a wise choice for someone to choose for a husband, but I was not a whole person by any means and did not think. I only groped along. I was sort of dead emotionally until I met Jim. He woke up a person inside me that I didn't know existed and from that second on all I wanted was Jim. I had just turned seventeen and Jim was twenty-seven.

From the minute I met Jim I started saving money. I wanted a place for us to be, a home. I worked three nights a week at a nursing home my senior year of High school and I saved everything I earned. I wanted a place of our own. It was an impossible dream.

Jim soon wound up in the county jail for several months, but I worked and waited. Then he got out and got into trouble again. This time I had to spend part of my savings for a lawyer. Jim went back to prison for a while. I was still working and saving but I didn't make much. But I didn't give up. I wanted nothing else.

I was a Christian and so was Jim, but we were still two complete messes. I knew that God knew how I felt, and I knew He was in this impossible dream of mine. I knew Jim was God's gift to me and me to him. But, without God we had no hope for a future.

After two years of saving money, Jim and I bought a small mobile home and got married. I wrote about our life and marriage in my first book, but I want to say again we had a lot of trouble. No one thought we would make it and they were right except for one thing. **GRACE. God's Grace.**

Neither Jim nor I were capable of supporting ourselves or in Jim's case of staying out of trouble, or in my case functioning as an adult. But God gave us miracle after miracle after miracle and sustained us. Not that it was easy, not even close.

As I reread my own book, I began to see something about my life. And it all came together as I was driving home from work in tears of gratitude and awe of God. I have lived my life by God's grace. It has been a life of grace. I had nothing else, no capability, no human help, no finances, no brains, no talent, nothing but brokenness, and God's grace.

I looked at my life, and even as it is, I realized God's grace had carried us through the years. We have had a wonderful life, only because of God's grace. He gave me everything I wanted, a life with Jim. I never lost him to prison even though I should have.

I thought about our life now. Jim and I have three wonderful grown children. All three serve the Lord and have all graduated from college. {Something Jim and I knew nothing about. I did not even know what a bachelor's degree was until my son got one.} I thought about the love and respect our kids show to their dad. {Ex- convicts don't get much respect]

Our son daily checks in on his dad to tell him he loves him usually with something for him, pizza or a hamburger or something delicious to eat. Our daughters shower him with love too. One pays for his membership to a near-by gym because he babysits for her so much, the other pampers him too.

We also have five grandchildren. I have to smile as I think of the seven and nine-year-old grandsons who walk in the door and make a bee line to grandpa's room. Grandpa usually has a new garage sale treasure for them or some candy or treat. Or the eleven-year-old granddaughter who tap tap taps on the door before bed to say goodnight to grandma and grandpa. {She stays here often}

As the tears flowed, I realized what was stirring in me. God was showing me something. My whole life has been about His grace. His grace has given me the impossible and although my life is not perfect, God has fulfilled the desires of my heart.

We would not have made it without grace. Time after time, through the years, it looked like we had come to the end, and that we were in too big a mess for even God to fix. But we saw Him come through over and over in miraculous ways, even though we were unimportant and broken and seemingly useless.

And now, as I looked ahead and realized that although life looks like it is over for us, it is not, because I am still depending on His grace. I know on my own I can't make it; I can't earn enough, or I am not healthy enough, but I never have been enough. The rest of my life will be lived by His grace! All my hope is in Him and in His grace.

My tears continued to flow. I knew God was beginning to teach me about His grace. I'd never thought too much about grace. It was one of those mystical words to me that I just wasn't sure I completely understood. But even though I did not understand it, He was showing me that I have lived it.

As I arrived home, my memory was being stirred. I have read and reread my favorite book, *The Final Quest,* by Rick Joyner, several times a year, and I had just reread it again. There is a line about grace in that book. I ran to my library and pulled it off the shelf and began to search. I had to read it again. I found it and read…." **You only have true strength to the degree that you walk in the grace of God,**

and 'He gives His grace to the humble'. No evil power can penetrate this mantle, because nothing can overpower His grace."

Suddenly God's grace seems like the most important thing in the world. Why had I not noticed this before? It was God's grace that got us through all those years.

I woke up again last night, I couldn't sleep. In the night I felt the Lord speaking to me in that ever so gentle voice, "Will you write a book about My grace?"

"Of course, Lord" I answered, "And I will write it by Your grace.

Chapter One

So Just What is Grace?

Amazing grace how sweet the sound

That saved a wretch like me

I once was lost but now I am found

Was blind but now I see

Twas grace that taught my heart to fear

And grace my fears relieved

How precious did that grace appear
The hour I first believed.

John Newton, 1779,

A definition of grace would be the unmerited favor of God.

Jesus died for us while we were yet sinners and made a way for us, God's grace. Haven't you heard that before? It sounds kind of religious and kind of nice, but a lot of us do not get it. The average person doesn't think about the grace of God. That is because we are out of reality! We do not even realize the fate that lies before us without God's grace. We live in la la land.

Howard Storm's Testimony

I saw a testimony on Christian television of a man named Howard Storm. It was very interesting. Howard was an educated man. He was the chairman of the art department at Northern Kentucky University.

But this man was an atheist and thought everyone who believed in God were idiots. He violently opposed religion and those who practiced religion. He says about himself he was not a very kind or happy person and used his rage to control and manipulate the people around him.

At the age of 38 Howard suffered from a perforated stomach and died in the hospital. As he was dying, he says, it never even occurred to him to pray. Howard found himself outside his body, looking at himself. He also saw his wife standing by his hospital bed and tried to speak to her. When she didn't answer he shouted profanities at her to get her to respond. But she could not hear him.

He was surprised to still be alive outside his body

because he thought death meant to cease to exist. But he found himself very much alive; in fact, his senses were heightened.

It was at this point some people called to him from the doorway. He thought they were doctors at first. He asked them who they were, but they were evasive in their answers, but they urged him to come, and hurry. Once in the hallway, he was surrounded by fog. These beings, he called them people, kept urging him on. Howard could not get a good look at them, but he could hear their voices, as they urged him to keep following them. He could see their forms like shadows only because they stayed fifteen or twenty feet in front of him in the haze.

Howard kept asking them questions, but their answers were very vague, they just kept urging him to follow. He began to follow for what seemed to be a long period of time, down this corridor that began to get darker, and the people no longer seemed as patient.

When Howard finally refused to go with them any longer, they showed their true nature. They were evil beyond imagination and lacked any kind of love or mercy at all. It was at this point they viciously attacked Howard and literally ripped him to pieces, toying with him in the most hideous and demeaning ways. With fiendish delight tore and bit his flesh until he was nothing but shreds. The more he tried to fight the more it delighted these hideous beings, and the more they overpowered and devoured him. When he gave up the struggle, in utter pain and exhaustion and he was no longer able to fight, they seemed to back off a bit.

This place Howard was in was very real and the pain and terror were beyond horrible. He realized this was his end and he thought it was worse than anything he could have ever imagined. He laid there, his flesh in pieces, in this place, and bleakly considered his future.

In this horrible state he thought of a little song he heard as a child. "Jesus loves me this I know for the Bible tells me so."

When he spoke the phrase of Jesus, his tormentors screamed and forbid him to use that name. Howard spoke anything he could remember, any phrase that had to do with God. "God bless America, the Lord is my Shepherd."

Finally, the evil beings fled.

Suddenly this man who despised God and religion clung to phrases he had heard as a child. The things he had so detested were now the only things that brought him any comfort whatsoever in this new existence he found himself in.

He never believed that anything he could not see existed but now found this afterlife was very real. He clung to any thought of God. It was no longer meaningless. In fact, it was the only thing that had any meaning. Then with his last ounce of strength he cried out with everything that was in his being, "Jesus save me!"

Howard cries out to the God he has so despised.

In this moment Howard saw a light like a comet in the distance move toward him. The light continued toward him, growing in brightness until it came to him and enveloped him in love. This being of light, which had come, simply when Howard called, was pure love and He picked Howard up and restored Howard's ripped and shredded flesh. Howard was so relieved and amazed he wanted to be with this being forever. This being was Jesus.

Grace.

Anything to do with God, Howard had always found meaningless, and he only believed in what he could see. He, like most on earth today, saw no value in grace or the sacrifice of Jesus Christ.   It simply didn't interest him, in fact, it enraged him. But his perspective changed. It was Howard's only hope, his last hope. Only when he saw the horror of the fate of being with those who, like him, despised God and had no love whatsoever; did he see the value of love and kindness. For Howard, somehow it was not too late. His life was not over.

What is Grace?

What is grace?
Grace is the unmerited favor of God, who in His love and mercy will forgive the vilest sinner because the sacrifice of Jesus who took their place. Grace is to stand perfect in the sight of God covered by this thing called grace. Grace changes us to the image of Christ, but also keeps us covered in perfect favor until that change is complete. Grace is mercy, grace is favor, and grace is love. Grace is a covering, a covering of our sin and nakedness

and shame. Grace is so powerful that murderers and thieves and those who have committed heinous crimes can call out for it and immediately be transformed by it.

Grace is only offered to humans on earth, the sons of Adam. And grace is only offered while we live this life. If we choose to reject this offer during our lifetime, or we simply ignore it, we will live eternally without grace.

Grace is the most valuable thing on earth. It is your greatest possession, and it fills your greatest need, the need for salvation. There is nothing on this earth more valuable than grace.

Just ask Howard!

Howard was obviously given a second chance at life. He is not the same man. He resigned his important college position and became a minister of the gospel he once so despised. He tells others in any way he can his story. He loves others and has devoted his life to keeping others from what was almost his fate.

Grace transforms. Howard was transformed, and he is continuing to be transformed into the image of Christ, the One who came to him when he called. And until that day Howard is completely transformed, Howard is perfect, in grace.

Summer Finds Grace

Howard's story reminds me a lot of my own; I like Howard could not stand hearing the gospel. It enraged me too. Just hearing about Jesus made me cringe, even though I was miserable.

I also, had come to a place in darkness, where I could see the ugliness of it, although unlike Howard I did not die to see where an eternity without God led, I felt like I was very close.

I feel like I came so close to falling headlong into the bottomless pit of an eternity in hell that I still inwardly gasp when I think about it. It only makes grace that much more precious to me.

Even though I was only fourteen when I came to the Lord, I was so deep in the grip of darkness I knew I did not have long to live. I could feel I was coming to an end.

I had embraced evil so thoroughly and then found it to be a nightmare. I was tormented. I was obsessed with suicide to end my misery, but I was too scared to do it, but I knew I would not live long the way I was treating my body.

I can see now, as I look back on those days, the grace at work in my life. The Lord successfully broke every bond that I had that would keep me from coming to Him. He showed me how meaningless I was to my so-called friends. He opened my eyes to my true spiritual condition. I was also being tormented by demons and evil no longer looked good to me at all.

Then He came and offered me love and grace. I also like Howard clung to Jesus. I found His love to be so wonderful I grabbed on and never let go. Jesus became the most beautiful word I had ever heard. It did not make me cringe anymore, in fact, just the opposite.

I wore a T-shirt with the word Jesus, on the front. I plastered Jesus stickers on anything they would stick to. I wore Jesus pins and doodled his name everywhere. Jesus, Jesus, Jesus! I wrote poems about Him and sang songs about Him. I hung pictures of Him all around my room. I lived walked and talked Jesus. I had my Bible tucked under my arm; I kept it school with me and read it all day long. Jesus now meant everything to me.

Amazing Grace

Is it no wonder that John Newton, who was once a very vile man and a former slave trader and the writer of the song, Amazing Grace, called grace amazing? He also knew the power of grace. He needed years of grace because his transformation from sinner to saint came slowly. But eventually John Newton became a minister of the gospel and the writer of the song *Amazing Grace.*

Grace is amazing. Grace is God's ability where our ability ends. Grace is God's strength when our strength ends, and God's grace contains all the power of God behind it.

What is grace? It is like the golden ticket. It means everything will work out for good. It opens doors that have been locked for ages. It gets us in to the throne of God with right standing. It is the covering, the blood of Jesus, which has been provided for us to save us from ourselves.

What is grace? It is the trump card. When Satan comes to steal, kill and destroy us and hell opens it evil jaws to swallow us, grace saves us. Grace tells the enemy to stand back and let us pass, we belong to Jesus now.

Grace covers us. It covers us in a clean white robe of righteousness and removes our filthy rags of sin.

It is undeserved.

Grace puts us in a state of eternal awe at the goodness of God. Grace is amazing.

Chapter Two

The Riches of His Grace

In Him we have redemption through His blood, the forgiveness of sins, in accordance with the riches of God's grace that He lavished on us with all wisdom and understanding. Ephesians 1:7 N.I.V.

In order that in the coming ages He might show the incomparable riches of His grace, expressed in His kindness to us in Christ Jesus. Ephesians 2:7

Scripture describes the riches of his grace as incomparable. In other words, there is nothing like them. The riches of His grace will take eons to discover so obviously I will not be able to cover them in one small chapter, not to mention I barely know what they are. But I will attempt to scratch the surface. Keep in mind these riches are not money. On an eternal timeline our currency is nearly worthless. These treasures of God's, the true riches, are unseen. I want to tell you about the treasure that I found.

His Kindness Towards Us

Because of the grace of God offered to us through Christ Jesus we will never know the judgement of God on us for our sins. We will only know His kindness. The richness of His grace is expressed in His kindness towards us. I don't know about you, but I value kindness very highly. In fact, as a child it made all the difference in the world to me.

As a child kindness was all that was important to me. My twin sister, Carol and I were born to a teenage mother, and we had no father. When we were quite tiny, we had an abusive stepfather who has left us emotional scars we both still live with.

As a small child, I valued kindness. When we were left with yet another babysitter the first thing that registered in my tiny mind was their level of kindness. In fact, that was all that mattered to me because I lived in a constant state of fear of the older people who had the power to hurt me.

It is uncanny to me, as an adult, the level of my ability so young to classify the adults around me. It wasn't measured in thoughts and words but rather levels of fear. I knew which babysitters were kind on the surface but really did not care. Others were evil beyond words and would abuse you and do things to you. Others were kind to you and actually cared.

Kindness came in levels.

Such as the lady that lived on the corner. She was the mother of one of our best friends. She was kind to us when we would play with her daughter. But one day on the way to school, the mean dog that lived across the street got off his chain.

We were walking to kindergarten and were right in front of her house when the dog started jumping on us. We were scared of dogs anyway, but this put us into hysterics. We hoped she would help us. I don't know if she was afraid also but even though she looked at us with compassion on her face she stood at her door and did nothing. She was kind but her kindness had limits. Everyone's did.

It only added to my confusion, why didn't people care?

I even knew the level of kindness of those people living in each house on my block. Some were safe to be around and were good to their own children but did not have time for someone else's children. Some had evil hearts and really cared for no one. One lady around the block was special. If you knocked on her door, she would let you in and give you a piece of candy.

The best place of all though was Grandma' and Grandpa's house. It was our safe place. The kindness meter went to the top and the fear level went to the bottom. But my grandparents were too old to watch us very often and still there was no adult I could actually go to for help. We did not hear the terms child abuse back then, and there were things too dark to talk about. And many times, although the babysitter wasn't kind, they weren't out right abusive, they just didn't care.

Kindness in others, especially adults was the thing I valued most.

The Kindness of God

My greatest joy and treasure in life was to discover the kindness of God. I was fourteen when I discovered it. That is when I gave my heart to the Lord. He reached out to me in such love and kindness as I had ever known. Never again did I have to search for kindness. I found it in God! He was better than grandma and grandpa! He became my safe place. Any time I needed Him I could run to him and hide myself in His kindness. Unlike people, His kindness was limitless.

I judged everyone on whether they were kind or not. Could they be trusted? I was disappointed until I found the kindness of God. He absolutely could be trusted. He loves me. He counts the hairs on my head. He puts my every tear in a bottle. He knows every one of my thoughts and He comes even before I call. The treasure of the grace of God is that it puts me in God's kindness; and His kindness is infinite.

Some may not see kindness as riches, but I do. It was the kind of riches I had been searching for my whole life, and through grace I found it.

More Riches, The Holy Spirit

Just before Jesus left earth, He told the disciples, *"But now I go away I go away to Him who sent Me, and none of you asks Me, 'Where are you going?' But because I have said these things sorrow has filled your heart. Nevertheless, I tell you it is to your advantage that I go away; for if I do not go away the Helper will not come to you; but if I depart, I will send Him to you." John 16:5-7*

Jesus told us it was better for us to have the Holy Spirit. The Holy Spirit was not given until after the resurrection of Jesus and Jesus departed back to heaven. This was something totally new. Something unheard of. Something that made even the angels stand back in awe. What is happening here?

The Holy Spirit is now dwelling in us. This not just the Holy Spirit moving into us, this is that, yes, but it is more. This is a real change. This event makes us a new creature, a new kind of being. Our spirit is joined with His Spirit. This is the mystery of God revealed. Through grace we have been transformed and reborn!

It happens inside our spirit, so it is not visible. The Holy Spirit is joined with our newly reborn spirit. Although it can't be seen in our realm it is still very real. But to those of us whom have had this event, of salvation, we know something has changed! Something is very different. We try to express it to others, but we don't know how to describe it with mere words. It transcends human understanding.

I went and announced to my friends, "I've got God now!" But they looked at me with dumbfounded faces. It was like I was speaking a foreign language; they did not know what I was saying.

But the change is there; it is real. We have new DNA, and we are a new creature. For now, the change is inside of us, but the day will come when the change will be evident.

In Him you also trusted, after you heard the word of truth, the gospel of your salvation; in whom also, having believed you were sealed with the Holy Spirit of promise, who is the guarantee of our inheritance until the redemption of the purchased possession, to the praise of His glory. Ephesians1:13-14

Many of the treasures of grace are hidden treasures, such as the Holy Spirit. Those who choose to follow God will have to walk by faith in this life. It has to do with the high calling we are called to. Even those of us who have come to the Lord, do not realize the treasure we carry inside us. We have the Spirit of God dwelling on the inside of us! This is an unbelievable treasure of grace!

The Attributes of Jesus

We have something else that comes through grace. The attributes of Jesus are part of the riches of grace. This is not something we do; it is what we become.

Jesus is love. The fruits of the spirit are the fruits of love. They are love, joy, peace patience kindness, gentleness, faithfulness and self-control.

We have the opportunity to become like Jesus. This is an unbelievable opportunity! If we choose to value the likeness of Jesus in this life, and we are willing to pay the price, we will receive this treasure and it will never be taken from us. The choice is ours how far into God we want to go. To become like Jesus, we choose to live like He lived.

The words of Jesus give us directions on how to live.

"But I say to you, love your enemies, bless those who curse you, do good to those who hate you, and pray for those who spitefully use you and persecute you." Matthew5:24

Of course that is only a small sample of His words.

To become like Jesus takes us on a narrow path that leads ever narrower. To truly become like Him takes being willing to follow that path. It is a humble path that does not follow selfish desires, but takes up our very own cross, just as Jesus did and we lay down our lives too.

It is our choice, to live like He lived but the reward of becoming like Him is phenomenal. It is an honor that is hard to be realized at this time. Again, it is hard to see the things that truly matter in the dim light of this world.

But Jesus lived for the invisible and so must we. We can actually become like Him.

The Storehouses of Heaven

The treasures of grace also provide for us on earth. Heaven has huge storehouses full of everything we could ever possibly need for our life on earth. Yes, this is for those of us still on earth. We can receive the things provided for us in this warehouse by faith. You don't have to try to talk God into any of it. He put it there for you. There are eyes for the blind and ears for the deaf. There are hearts and lungs and livers and kidneys. There are other things too, balms and potions that give strength and hope and even a little something to help you sleep.

God has exactly what you need, prepared for you, for exactly when you need it. He has great storehouses in heaven, and he owns the cattle on a thousand hills on earth. {In other words, He owns everything] He also makes arrangements for your needs to be met on earth.

We receive His provision by faith. We are to live by faith.

Citizenship

Through grace we receive citizenship to God's kingdom. This is the golden ticket. To have citizenship there is beyond your wildest dreams. To those on earth who have citizenship there this means a place is being prepared for them. The homes in heaven are exquisite, and they are designed to the tastes of those who own them. Those who love the mountains will have a home built up in the mountains. Our golfers may have a whole golf course on their grounds. And that is just the beginning, there are many delightful places to visit. If you enjoy traveling on earth the travel in heaven is far above that!   To those who receive the grace of God you have citizenship in this wonderful place.

Angels

Have you ever seen these people who are so rich they have a staff who take care of things. They have bodyguards and drivers and people who do things for them. We are like them.

Our Father has a whole staff of angels that look out for us. There are some that stay with us all the time and some that are sent to us on special assignments. Again, this is something that is not openly visible. But just about everyone has an angel story or two.

I just had an angel experience a couple of nights ago. My husband Jim, who frequently suffers depression rolled over in the middle of the night and said to me, "We are all alone."

"No, we are not." I answered him, hoping to cheer him up, "there are angels here with us."

When I said that, I saw what looked sort of like a window open and an angel's head popped through. The angel said to me, "Yeah, there are six of us here."

When I told Jim what I saw, all six angels started cheering, they were just as glad I could see them as I was. Then they gave me some instructions, on how to help Jim.

God loves us so much He assigns angels to each of us.

True Riches

You may have noticed that all these things that I have mentioned are not things that we can see on earth. That is because true riches are eternal things. The things on earth that many people lie and cheat and even kill for are only shadows of riches. In a sense they are so temporal that they are not even real.

The whole world is caught up in pursuit of these shadows and the true riches do not appeal to them. Many Christians also use their faith to try to acquire these shadows instead of fixing their eyes above on true riches.

The most valuable things are unseen, which we already discussed, such as love and the attributes of Jesus. Many in the Bible, whose stories have been written for us, are examples to us of those who have followed true riches.

The Early Church Valued True Riches

The early church in the book of Acts saw the value in these kinds of riches. Suddenly their houses and land didn't mean anything to them anymore. Something else had much greater value.

Selling their possessions and goods, they gave to anyone as he had a need. Every day they continued to meet together in the temple courts. They broke bread in their homes and ate together with glad and sincere hearts, praising God and enjoying the favor of all people. And the Lord added to their number daily those who were being saved. Acts 2:45-47

*All the believers were one in heart and mind. No one claimed that any of his possessions was his own, but they shared everything they had. With great power the apostles continued to testify to the resurrection of the Lord Jesus, and **much grace was upon them all.** There were no needy persons among them. From time to time those who owned lands or houses sold them, brought the money from the sales and put it at the apostle's feet and it was distributed to anyone as he had need. Acts4:32-35 NIV*

What has happened to these people? They do not value temporal things anymore. And as they are laying down their worldly riches, they are gaining the unseen riches and they are receiving a greater measure of grace.

Let's look at this again and see what kind of riches they have.

One day Peter and John were going up to the temple at the time of prayer- at three in the afternoon. Now a man crippled from birth was being carried to the temple gate called Beautiful where he was put every day to beg from those going into the temple courts. When he saw Peter and John about to enter, he asked them for money. Peter looked straight at him as did John.

Then Peter said, "Look at us!" So, the man gave them his attention, expecting to get something from them. Then Peter said, "Silver or gold I do not have, but what I have I give to you. In the name of Jesus Christ of Nazareth, walk."

Taking him by the right hand, he helped him up, and instantly the man's feet and ankles became strong. He jumped to his feet and began to walk. Then he went with them into the temple courts, walking and jumping and praising God, they recognized him as the same man who used to sit begging at the temple gate Beautiful, and they were filled with wonder and amazement at what happened to him. Acts 3:1-10 NIV

Peter and John are giving beggars something better than money! They are passing out the riches of God's grace. They have tapped into the supply of God available to them through grace. And that supply is exactly what is needed, for exactly who needs it, exactly when it's needed. In this case a lame man was miraculously healed. The riches of grace are true riches. The true riches of grace are unseen because they are from the age to come, eternity. And they prepare us for the age to come. They transport us from the earthly to the heavenly. They give us standing as Christ, in the eternal realm.

Grace gives us what we need when we need it.

It is the strength of Samson when we are weak.

It can open up a path in the sea so you can walk through on dry land; just ask Moses and the children of Israel.

It can stop the sun from going down, when you need more time, just ask Joshua and the armies of Israel. Or it can cause the sun dial to go backwards, just ask Hezekiah.

Or ask Shadrach Meshach and Abednego about how grace can cause flames not to burn you; or Daniel how it shuts the mouths of lions.

God's grace is rich, it gives you what you need when you need it and it's always on time. It's an ark in a flood, a great fish when you're drowning or an army of angels when you are surrounded by enemies.

It can feed five thousand men with a little boy's lunch, find your tax money in a fish's mouth, or give you a drink of water from a rock.

It heals the sick, cleanses lepers and raises the dead.

The riches of God's grace are endless. The vast storehouses of heaven are filled with them. They are provided for each need that ever was or will be, and they are provided for us by grace. These are true riches.

Chapter Three

The Price of Grace

Surely, He took up our infirmities and carried our sorrows, yet we considered Him stricken by God, smitten by Him and afflicted. But He was pierced for our transgressions, He was crushed for our iniquities; the punishment that brought us peace was upon Him, and by His wounds we are healed. We all like sheep, have gone astray, each of us has turned to his own way; and the Lord has laid on Him the iniquity of us all. Isaiah 53:4-6NIV

God made Him who had no sin to be sin for us, that in Him we might become the righteousness of God. 2 Corinthians 5:21NIV

I work as a home health aide, taking care of people in their homes. Sometimes while I am working, I get exposed to things on television that I would never ever watch. That just happened two nights ago. A patient was watching a show that I found horribly offensive. It was a military detective show; but it was very graphic. In it were crime scenes with mutilated bodies, and grisly murder scenes. I stayed as busy as I could, but I could not leave the patient. I tried to block out the television by staying busy, but still I was exposed to it. I felt violated and sick. That is an understatement.

I felt traumatized by the filthy, foul, gross, things that were displayed on that television show. I felt angry and defiled. Have you ever been so grossed out that you just felt rage at wickedness? I did. I wanted out of there. It was like being vomited on.

This happens to me. I have sheltered myself from worldly entertainment and I can tolerate very little of it. I despise most movies and television shows. They gross me out. And at work, through no fault of my own I become defiled.

One time I had a different patient who was watching a movie about magicians. It gave me a very evil feeling. That night when I went to bed, I had a nightmare about it. I dreamt I had a clean bowl and my patient put a slimy creature in it.

When I woke up the Lord spoke to me and told me that I had to stop working on writing my books for a while. That movie had defiled me. I felt horrible. Sin is so disgusting.

This in a very, very small way could describe how Jesus felt. He knew no sin, yet He became sin for us. Jesus, through love for us, took on all the sin, ever committed by human beings. Jesus who was pure, He had never committed a single sin, took on every foul filthy degenerate disgusting sin ever done. He carried them and He paid the price for them. Jesus had to become something repulsive and filthy and foul.

This was a horrible thing for Him to face.

He also faced every evil wicked and vile spirit including Satan and was tempted by Him, not as God but as a man in a tired, hungry body. He fasted in the wilderness for forty days and then was tempted by Satan. To say this was unpleasant is a huge understatement.

What is the price of sin?

The price of sin is the second death. It is eternal death. It is unending torment in the Lake of Fire and eternal separation from God. When God turns His back, and rejects a soul, they are eternally doomed. There is no more hope, and all life and joy are ended. There is nothing worse, nothing. Jesus had to face this for us; God turned His back on Jesus. The Bible describes the second death.

Then I saw a great white throne and Him who sat on it, from whose face the earth and the heaven fled away. And there was found no place for them. And I saw the dead, small and great, standing before God, and books were opened. And another book was opened, which is the

Book of Life. And the dead were judged, each one according to his works, by the things that were written in the books. The sea gave up the dead who were in it, and Death and Hades delivered up the dead who were in them. And they were judged, each one according to his works. Then Death and Hades were cast into the lake of fire. This is the second death. And anyone not found written in the Book of Life was cast into the lake of fire. Revelation 20:11-15NKJ

This is what we deserve. This is the death Jesus had to face for us, the second death. This is the price for sin. Obviously, the way I feel about sin is in a small way like God. He will not tolerate sin. He will judge and burn sin forever.

So, Jesus had to take on the sin of the world and He had to taste the second death for us. Jesus had to carry the sin of the world. He had to be rejected by God and He had to be taken captive by Satan. Now, add to that the normal stuff, the stuff we could see, the extreme torture, the physical pain and the brutal death of crucifixion. That is the price of sin.

The Weight of Sin

We see the weight of sin falling on Jesus as He enters the Garden of Gethsemane to pray. Something begins to happen to Jesus. The Book of Matthew states *He began to be sorrowful and deeply distressed.*

The ugliness of sin is literally coming on Jesus and killing Him prematurely. Jesus is overcome with sorrow. He needs help.

At this point Jesus takes Peter, James and John and says to them, *"My soul is exceedingly sorrowful, even to death. Stay here and watch with Me."*

Jesus is in deep distress, so much so He is dying. He even begins to sweat drops of blood.This is a real condition called Hematidrosis. Hematridrosis is a rare condition in which a person will sweat blood and it is caused by acute fear and extreme mental stress.

Something extremely horrific is beginning to happen to Jesus in the garden. Jesus is suffering deeply. He is feeling acute fear and extreme mental stress. This is Jesus, the same one who stopped the storms, faced crowds that wanted stone him, drove the money changers from the temple and cast out legions of demons from the demoniac. Jesus is fearless. So, what is happening to Him in the garden that is so horrible? The weight of sin is falling on Him.

He is actually so distressed He is at the point of death. At one point an angel comes to strengthen Him so He can continue on to the cross.

This is the price of grace, but it is only just beginning, Jesus ordeal has only just begun. He is beginning to feel the weight of our sin. He was beginning to feel the horrors of the damned. Every atrocity ever committed was being laid on His soul as He was beginning to bear the sin of the world. He turns to His dearest friends Peter, James and John for help, but they fall asleep.

The Red Stone

Rick Joyner describes in his book, *The Final Quest,* a vision where he experiences some of the suffering of Christ.

In this book, Rick tells how he is in a prophetic vision and experiencing the treasures of salvation. Rick is in a room that is so large it seems to be without end. As he enters the room the glory is so stunning, he falls to his knees. The floor of the room was silver, the pillars were gold and the ceiling diamond. The room was filled with angels in various uniforms. He sees stones of various colors in the room. An angel explains that they are the treasures of salvation.

The first two stones he touches are blue and green and when he touches it, he experiences revelations of the tree of life and creation. As he touches each stone, the revelation contained in that stone is what he experiences. Just by touching these two stones his comprehension of God and His universe grows substantially.

I want to quote for you what happens when he touches the red stone. He grabs the red stone suddenly, looking for comfort, because he has a terrifying experience when he stands in front of the door that leads to the Judgement seat of Christ. I will quote the book. These are clips from the book that pertain to the red stone.

I turned away from that door and retreated fast. There was a beautiful red stone nearby, which I almost

lunged at to lay my hands on. Immediately I was in the Garden of Gethsemane beholding the Lord in prayer. The agony I beheld was even more terrible than the door I had just seen. Shocked, I jerked my hand away from the stone and fell down in exhaustion.

Rick asks a nearby angel about it.

"When you touch the stones, we are able to see a little of what you see and feel a little of what you feel," said the angel. "We know that all these stones are great treasures, and all of the revelations they contain are priceless. We beheld for a moment the agony of the Lord before His crucifixion, and we felt briefly what He felt that terrible night. It is hard for us to understand how our God could ever suffer like that. It makes us appreciate much more what an honor it is to serve the men for whom He paid such a terrible price."

Rick decides to return to the stone.

The time I spent at the red stone was the most painful that I have ever experienced. Many times, I just could not take anymore but had to withdraw my hand. Several times I went back to the blue or green stones to rejuvenate my soul before I returned. It was harder to return to the red stone each time, but my love and appreciation for the Lord was growing more through this than anything I had ever learned or experienced.

Finally, when the Father departed from Jesus on the cross, I could stand it no longer. I quit.

I just laid prostrate on the floor. I was weeping over what the Lord had gone through. I wept also because I knew I had deserted Him just like His disciples. I

failed Him when He needed me the most, just like they did.

Although Rick does not describe in this book, the suffering of Christ, he does describe how painful it was to behold. Jesus suffering was intense. Rick is beholding the agony the Lord is experiencing to carry the weight of our sin. What he sees is so terrible he falls prostrate on the floor, and he is weakened. The angels with Rick are also shocked and astounded, as they also see what Rick is seeing.

It has to be this way. This is the heavy price of grace. This is for you. This is all for you. You may not know it now, but someday you will, this is your greatest treasure. Christ suffering for you. Nothing else will ever come close. Jesus so loves us; He literally was crushed for us. It had to be; for the price of grace.

In the Garden of Gethsemane Jesus' soul began to suffer unspeakable horror. But this was just the beginning. The crowds of those who want Jesus put to death appear and take Jesus by force. They are being egged on by the forces of darkness that rule this world.

Satan and every evil being have descended. They are all here in Jerusalem, on this night. They begin to incite and possess all they can as their evil hordes descend to devour Jesus.

This demonic army attacks unhindered, this is their hour. Michael, the ruler of the angelic armies and all the millions of angels in his army, reluctantly stand back. They have been ordered by God to let the evil horde through. The angels stand back in horror as Jesus is seized by this army of evil, seen and unseen. They do not understand why, but Jesus has to face this completely alone, they can only watch, they may not help.

Pilate's Account to Rome

In the book, *The Archko Volume,* there is given an account of Pilate's written report to Rome of Jesus death. These are official documents that were copied from the vaults at the Vatican in Rome in the 1800's. I want to quote to a portion of Pilate's report that describes that rage unleashed upon Jesus. Pilate sensed the spirit realm accurately as he describes the mood.

"Often in our civil commotions have I witnessed the furious anger of the multitude, but nothing compared to what I witnessed on this occasion. It might have been truly said that all the phantoms of the infernal regions had assembled at Jerusalem. The crowd appeared not to walk, but to be borne off and whirled as a vortex, rolling along in living waves from the portals of the praetorium even unto Mount Zion, with such howling screams, shrieks and vociferations such as were never heard in the seditions of the Pannonia, or in the tumults of the forum.

"By degrees the day darkened like a winter's twilight, such as had been at the death of the great Julius Caesar. It was likewise the Ides of March. I, the continued governor of a rebellious province, was leaning against a column of my basilica, contemplating athwart the deary gloom these fiends of Tartarus dragging to execution the

innocent Nazarene. All around me was deserted. Jerusalem had vomited forth her indwellers through the funeral gate that leads to Gemonica. An air of desolation and sadness enveloped me. My guards had joined the cavalry and the centurion, with a display of power, was endeavoring to keep order. I was left alone, and my breaking heart admonished me that what was passing at that moment appertained rather to the history of the gods than that of men. A loud clamor was heard proceeding from Golgotha, which, borne on the winds, seemed to announce an agony such as was never heard by mortal ears. Dark clouds lowered over the pinnacle of the temple and setting over the city covered it as with a veil. So dreadful were the signs men saw both in the heavens and on the earth that Dionysius the Aeropagite is reported to have exclaimed, "Either the author of nature is suffering, or the universe is falling apart."

Pilate's account is very descriptive of the fury unleashed from hell and carried out upon the body of Jesus. The evil descending on Jesus was apparent. Even nature reacts to the fury being unleashed upon Jesus, its Creator, as the sun darkens, and gloom descends and even at one point the earth shook. All of hell has gathered together to unleash their fury on Jesus. It is no wonder His body was wounded beyond description.

The Wounds of Christ

I also want to talk about the suffering Jesus

experienced in His body. Immediately after Jesus was seized in the Garden His physical suffering began.

Jesus was seized by the religious leaders who were looking to put Him to death. He was slapped and spit on. Then they blindfolded Him and as they hit Him, they taunted, "Prophesy to us Christ! Who is the one who struck you?"

This continued until morning when they brought Him to Pilate.

Pilate had Jesus scourged.

The Shroud of Turin, which I believe to be authentic, shows the extent of the damage the scourging did to Jesus' body. From the shroud we can see the damage done by the whipping. I will quote an examination from the shroud.

There are over 100 scourge marks on the man's front and back. The marks are more prevalent on the back side and run in groups of two or three. The marks run horizontal and diagonal and vary in light contusions to deep punctures.

The scourging was done with a three-pronged whip with pieces of metal tied in. Jesus was given thirty-nine lashes. Jesus has scourge marks predominantly on his back but also on His legs and even some around the front of His body. He is literally ripped to shreds.

Now comes the part that bothers me the most, the Roman guards. I am going to quote Matthew for this part.

Then the soldiers of the governor took Jesus into the Praetorium and gathered the whole garrison around Him. And they stripped Him and put a scarlet robe on Him.

When they had twisted a crown of thorns, they put it on His head, and a reed in His right hand. And they bowed the knee before Him and mocked Him, saying, "Hail the King of the Jews!" Then they spat on Him and took the reed and struck Him on the head. And when they had mocked Him, they took the robe off Him, put His own clothes on Him and led Him away to be crucified. Matthew 27:27-31

The reason this part bothers me so is these were depraved men who regularly made sport of their victims and took delight in it. Jesus was stripped and taunted. These were degenerate men who took great delight in every kind of torment. God only knows what all happened to Him at this point.

Now we have new wounds on Jesus body. He has a crown of thorns twisted into His brow and he has been beaten with a reed. This is also visible on the shroud. The image of Jesus on the shroud shows considerable swelling of Jesus face. He is swollen above and below His eyes, His cheeks and the cartilage in His nose is split. And of course, the crown of His head took many punctures from the hideous crown of thorns.

Jesus is ripped to shreds and swollen and beaten to the point He is unrecognizable.

Just as many were astonished at you, So His visage was marred more than any man and His form more than the sons of men Isaiah 52:14

As Jesus was led out to be crucified He did carry His cross at first we know this because of the wounds on the tops His shoulders visible from the Shroud. Then Simon of Cyrene was forced to carry the cross. At some point here

Jesus beard was pulled out in the center. This is also visible from the shroud.

Next Jesus is nailed to the cross. He receives nail wounds through His wrists and through His feet. His last wound is after His death a spear mark on His side.

Jesus is pulverized. All this has been demonically inspired. Satan and his minions have enraged the crowd feverishly. No movie has ever shown the extent of the wounds of Jesus. He has been beaten continually all night and day. He is beaten and wounded on every part of His body from His head to his feet. Jesus has never done any wrong and yet such fury is carried out on His body that He Has been cut to ribbons.

The Father Turns His Back

Jesus hung on the cross for about six hours. He was crucified at about nine o'clock in the morning and He died around three o'clock in the afternoon. From about noon to about three o'clock the sky became dark. At three o'clock the Roman soldiers came to break Jesus legs to speed up His death but to their surprise Jesus was already dead. This is when one of the soldiers stabbed Jesus in His side with his spear and blood and water flowed out of Jesus side.

As Jesus hung on the cross with the weight of the sin on Him, and as people mocked and scoffed, the unthinkable happened to Jesus. The Father turned His back and Jesus was separated from God. Jesus tasted the second death.

I believe Jesus died of a broken heart. So great was His pain when the Father turned His back on Him. The eternal love between Jesus and the Father is so great, this pain is almost too much for Jesus to bear. His heart bursts.

And about the ninth hour Jesus cried out with a loud voice, saying "Eli, Eli lama sabachthani?" That is, "My God, My God, why have You forsaken Me?" Some of those who stood there, when they heard that said, "This man is calling for Elijah!"

Immediately one of them ran and took a sponge, filled it with sour wine and put it on a reed and offered it to Him to drink. The rest said, "Let him alone; let us see if Elijah comes to save Him."

And Jesus cried out again with a loud voice and yielded up his spirit. Matthew 27:45-50

As Jesus died some tremendous things were happening in the spirit realm. The signs were being seen in nature. For three hours as Jesus is on the cross the sky is dark. Then as Jesus enters the belly of the earth, the earth literally shakes. There is an earthquake. The Bible tells us: *Then behold, the veil of the temple was torn in two from top to bottom; and the earth quaked and rocks were split, and the graves were opened; and many graves of the saints who had fallen asleep were raised; and coming out of the graves after the resurrection, they went into the holy city and appeared to many. Matthew 27:51-53*

As Jesus entered hell it caused an earthquake and graves were opened.

Jesus in Hell

Jesus' ordeal is not yet over. Jesus now faces hell. Jesus not only went to hell; He went to the lowest deepest part of hell. He had to; He had to go into the lowest place.

Satan and his myriads of evil beings pounced on Jesus with fiendish delight. They took out their hatred on Him, as He took our place in hell.

Satan has fallen from heaven and there will never be for him the chance to repent. His rage toward God and Jesus up until now has been carried out upon humans; God of course is unreachable, until now.

Satan is delighted at Jesus misfortune; he wonders how Jesus could have allowed Himself to get in this weak position. He has laid aside His deity and become human. Satan sees the love of God for mankind as supreme weakness. Now he has Jesus as his prisoner and in his pride, he sees himself as the victor. Every spirit and evil being of the fallen world have united together to vent their extreme rage at their eternal loss on Jesus, and their glee that He is now theirs to unleash their rage upon. They have been throughout this entire ordeal as they railed at him and ripped His flesh through fallen man. But now they have Him in their domain. They pounce on Him in all their wickedness.

In utter humility, Jesus stands alone against them, completely alone.

On the third day in the morning, something happens. A great flash of light fills the regions of darkness.

The bowels of the earth shake, and the darkness's flee in terror. Jesus bursts forth from the grave with resurrection power carrying the keys to death and hell. His body and His spirit reunite, and Jesus is alive.

Satan overplayed his hand because Jesus ascended from hell, in victory, and filled all things. He has successfully paid the price for grace.

Therefore He says;
"When He ascended on high, He led captivity captive, and he gave gifts to men." {Now this, "He ascended"—what does it mean but that He also first descended into the lower parts of the earth? He who descended is also the One who ascended far above all the heavens, that He might fill all things.} Ephesians 4:8-10

Jesus submitted Himself to hell for a time and all the horrors that go with it. But then Jesus arose from hell defeating death and hell and the grave. This was also felt on earth in the form of another great earthquake. Then Jesus body resurrected with a great light because His form was photographed onto the shroud as a perfect negative. He laid aside His grave clothes and after appearing to the Mary's, He ascended to heaven.

Jesus Now

So now that Jesus has been resurrected and His physical suffering is over, does that mean all His suffering is over?

Well, no it is not.

Jesus body is resurrected and is healed; even though He still bears His scars, but Jesus is still suffering in the deepest part of Him, in His heart. Not only is Jesus suffering, but we His body, His people will share in His sufferings.

How is Jesus still suffering?

Jesus has become Our Savior, Our Mediator. He is the only hope that mankind has. Jesus is literally in love with mankind. He was poured out and crushed for us, but now He lives for us. He carries our sorrows and burdens still.

Jesus suffers every time a child is abused or cold or hungry or unloved. He sees the children, little girls and boys forced into prostitution, everyone. Jesus still suffers. He feels the pain of every child in the womb, whose life is ripped from them in the most horrific manner. He sees the elderly, the lonely and the forgotten. He sees the forsaken wife or husband, the cheated, the abandoned. This is how He suffers still; He feels every pain every tear and every sorrow of mankind. He has joined Himself with us and He will never forsake us.

He also sees those who suffer for Him, who endure persecution for righteousness sake like He did. He also sees those in hell, and He mourns for them because He has already done all He could do for them. He loves us, He cries with us, and He is ever present with us.

I often thought in my life, "Dying doesn't scare me, living does."

Life is scary and painful. There have been many times I have wished it was over and have begged God to take me. I was under the misguided thought that Jesus is in heaven, He does not know how awful it is to live on earth. But I was wrong.

Jesus is still in pain because He lives for us and with us. He lives our pain, our suffering and our sorrow. He carries us still. He is our high priest; He is our Mediator. His job is not done yet. He is doing the hard thing; He is living, and He is living with each of us.   Jesus hasn't left us. He has promised to always be with every one of us. He is still paying the price of offering us grace.

This is My Glory

The cross of Christ is my glory!

Why would I say such a thing? Do I take pleasure in the suffering of Christ?

Absolutely not. But it is precious to me. It is precious because it is the price that was paid for me. It is precious because it is the depth of love that Jesus has for me. It was the price of the grace that has been offered to me.

There have been times in my life that I have suffered, a lot. I tell about my life in my book, *The Impossible Marriage.* I married an ex-convict who was also an alcoholic. I had some miserable times. Sometimes I was so distressed I could not even pray. But I could picture the cross and Jesus in agony. In fact, because of my own agony it was very easy to picture Jesus on the cross in agony. In fact, it was so real I felt as if I was there. I placed myself there before His cross and we suffered together. But my suffering did not compare to His suffering. But His suffering brought me great comfort. Even on the cross, Jesus comforts me. His love is so great.

Even Rick, further on in his book, *The Final Quest* receives comfort from the suffering of Christ. I will quote that segment for you.

I was in the most frightening darkness I had ever experienced. To take each step became a terrible battle with fear. Soon I began to think that I had stepped into hell itself. Finally, I decided to retreat, but when I turned to go back, I could not see anything. The door closed and I could not see where it was located. I started to feel that everything that had happened to me, and everything that had been said to me by the eagles and angels had been a ruse to trap me in this hell. I had been deceived!

I cried to the Lord to forgive me and help me. Immediately I began to see Him on the cross, just as when I had laid my hand on the red stone in the chamber I had just left. Again, I beheld the darkness of His soul as he stood alone bearing the sin of the world. In that chamber this had been a terrible darkness to behold, but now it was a light. I resolved to go on, fixing my mind on Him.

Jesus suffering was so intense it becomes a light in Rick's darkness, just like it had become for me. His suffering was literally for me, it was literally for Rick, and it is literally for you. It is light in our greatest darkness. His cross is our glory, and the glory is the depth of His love for us.

Jesus had a huge price to pay but it was necessary. All of it was necessary.

The Price of Grace

The price of grace was and is very high. But so are the riches of grace, they are vast. Jesus made the final sacrifice when He became sin for us. He still bears the scars. And He still suffers every time someone He loves suffers. He has attached Himself to you. He carries your burdens, your sorrows, yes and even your joys. Jesus did not stop on the day of resurrection. He ever lives to make intercession for you. The price of grace was paid for because of love. It is a love that we can never fathom. It is a love that bore unbelievable suffering and sacrifice. It is also a love that will continue on for all eternity. The price of grace that was paid for you is not to be taken lightly. It is holy. In fact, there is nothing more holy. We are to treat it with awe.

Chapter Four

God Has a Plan for Your Life

For we are God's workmanship, created in Christ Jesus to do good works, which God prepared in advance for us to do. Ephesians 2:10

God has a part for you to play in His plan. God has a divine plan for your life which will bring His good to earth through you. You were created with a destiny planted inside of you. You have been given what you need to do what God has foreordained you to do. He has put in you irrevocable gifts for that very purpose. He has placed you in the location you need to be and caused you to be born at the right time. There is a part in the divine scheme of the universe that you are created and equipped to fill and if you do not fulfill your role, it won't get done. There are people who need you, there are events for you to fulfill. If you are willing and you give yourself to God, you can be an instrument in the mighty hand of God.

A Visit to God's Throne Room

In the book *Angels on Assignment* Pastor Roland Buck describes a visit to God's throne room. Roland was sitting at his desk, on a January night in 1977, preparing his Sunday sermon when he heard a voice call him. "Come with Me into the throne room where the secrets of the universe are kept."

At this point Roland was pulled upward to heaven for a wonderful visit with God. Roland was taught many things. During Roland's visit with God, he was allowed to ask questions. Roland asked God if He really made individual plans for each and every life. Roland says he had felt this job would be too big for even God to fill.

In response to Roland's question God showed Roland the files of each life. There were billions of them! The vastness caused Roland's head to swim. Then God did a very surprising thing. He pulled out Roland's file and wrote down for him to see 120 events that would happen in Roland's life from his file. Everything on the paper was immediately imprinted on Roland's mind.

Then God continued to show Roland how He has a plan for each life. He pulled out the files for many different lives and showed Roland that He had a blueprint for each person's life. One such file was for the apostle Paul. Paul's blueprint revealed that Paul would be used to bring the gospel to kings and rulers and men of authority. God prepared Paul for this task by giving him an intelligent mind and caused him to study under the greatest scholars of his day. God had chosen Paul to write the scripture, so through Paul's life God had prepared him for this task.

When Roland returned to his life after his time with God, the 120 things on his list began happening just as he had seen in heaven. Many of the events were encounters with people. He had a woman come to his office who had been involved in witchcraft, just as he had seen on his list, and he recognized her immediately. Roland ministered to her, and she was set free.

Event number four on his list had to do with a man who would come to the Lord on February 4, 1977, but would die on May, 30th of the same year, in a plane crash. He came to the Lord right on schedule and a week before he died, he asked to see Roland. The man told Roland he had a feeling he was going to die soon. Roland could not reveal to him what he knew but he told the man all about heaven, just as he asked. The next week as he was foretold on his list the man was killed in a plane crash.

Item number 63 on Roland's list he had seen in much detail. It concerned a couple with marital problems that would come to his office for help. When they did not show up at the appointed time from the list, Roland wondered what happened and stayed at his office past closing time and waited. The phone rang and a man's voice asked him if he could come immediately. He did not identify himself. When the man and his wife came into his church office Roland surprised them by greeting them by name. Then the couple told Roland that they had been having trouble in their marriage and they had been fighting. They had driven around and stopped at a motel to try to work things out and had seen his ad for counseling in the yellow pages in the motel. That is why they called. But they assured Roland that after they had a long talk, they had worked things out and they no longer needed his services.

Roland knew better because he had seen this event before it happened in God's throne room. He said "No, things are not okay." Then he turned to the wife, "You have a gun in your purse, and you are planning to shoot your husband when you return to your motel room."

The husband was alarmed and started shouting to his wife, "You better not shoot me!" The woman was also alarmed and began to shake. She opened her purse and handed Roland the gun and both the husband and wife fell down on their knees and called out to God. Roland had seen all this on his list.

Roland's list was only a tiny slice from his file in heaven. God had many things ordained for him to do; this was just a little example God let him see to prove a point and answer his question to God, "Does he really have a plan for each individual life?"

Each person on earth has a file in heaven with a divine plan for their life. Whether or not we fulfill it is up to us. God's perfect plan involves us being aware of those God brings into our lives for a reason.

Jesus Follows the Father's Plan

Jesus did not do what He felt like doing when He was on the earth. He followed the Father's plan for His life, just like He expects us to do.

I tell you the truth, the Son can do nothing by Himself, He can only do what He sees the Father doing, because whatever the Father does the Son also does. John 5:19

Nothing was done by accident. Jesus followed the divine plan for His life. He laid down His will and chose to be used by the Father.

Jesus fulfilled His divine appointments. He had many, the woman at the well, Zacchaeus the wee little man in the sycamore tree, the lame man by the pool, the demon possessed man and even Satan in the wilderness. Everything He did was the Fathers plan. Some of the things that happened in Jesus life were prophesied hundreds of years ahead of time in the Old Testament. Nothing was done on His own. And Jesus fulfilled all that He was supposed to do while on the earth. There is layer upon layer upon layer of truth and meaning in every miracle Jesus did.

God had a divine plan for Jesus life. Even the things that didn't seem very divine, like being born in a stable because there was no room in the Inn. There were plenty of times that didn't seem so divine, fleeing to Egypt to avoid being killed by Herod, storms, trials and persecutions. How would you like to fast in a desert for forty days? But Jesus in His short thirty-three and a half years on earth fulfilled everything that needed to be fulfilled. He paid the price for every need of mankind. He delivered us with His obedience. He carried out perfectly a divine plan laid out for Him by the Father and He successfully redeemed mankind and destroyed the works of Satan for those who would choose to follow Him.

Jesus succeeded in fulfilling His mission on earth and provided for us, salvation, healing for our bodies and healing for our minds and emotions. He left us His peace. He showed us how to love, taught us to forgive and gave us an example to follow. He taught us what to value, where to keep our treasure and how to not to worry and to trust. He gave us an example of humility, of emptying Himself and laying down His life for others. He showed us unbelievable things. He became angry yes; when the things of God were being perverted and He threw the money changers out of the temple. But He also forgave the sinners and the adulteress, and the tax collectors considered to be the vilest of sinners. (Who likes the IRS?]

Jesus life was divinely planned to meet our every need. Your life is also divinely planned, also. Before the world was created your life was carefully, lovingly, divinely planned.

All the days ordained for me were written in your book before one of them came to be Psalms 139:16

A Prostitute Finds God's Plan

I recently saw a wonderful example of someone finding God's plan for their life on the television show, *It's*

Supernatural, with the host Sid Roth. This particular show Sid had a guest named Shawn Bolz. Shawn is used by God in wonderful ways. On the show Shawn told Sid about an experience he had recently had.

Shawn was visiting Hawaii and was out for a walk one evening to get a sandwich. He was staying in a nice place, but it was near the red-light district. As he was walking, he was approached by a man who asked him, "Do you want a girl?"

The man pointed to a young girl who was about sixteen years old sitting on some steps between two teen age boys. Shawn's heart was grieved for her; she was obviously a runaway living on the streets. So, he approached her to talk to her. Shawn told the young girl he was a pastor, and a Christian and then he explained to her God had a plan for her life that he made millions of years ago. He also asked her what she wanted to do with her life.

"I don't know," the young girl replied.

"Close your eyes and pray this prayer," Shawn told her, "God, I know you have thought of me for millions of years and that you have a plan for my life." As Shawn prayed the young girl repeated the words after him. "Show me the plan for my life that would bring you the most joy."

Suddenly the girl let out a startled cry, and then shrieked, "I heard something, I am supposed to be a cook!"

"Do you like to cook?" Shawn asked her.

"I don't know" the startled girl replied.

"All right," Shawn began again, "I want you to ask

God one step for your life that you can make toward being a cook."

As the girl prayed again and then picked up her head, "I think I am supposed to call my uncle. He owns a diner. I think he would let me work there and I think he would also give me a place to sleep."

Shawn encouraged the girl to call her uncle and he also gave her his own phone number and asked her to keep in touch. Then he left.

Six months later he received a call from this young girl. She had gone to work at her uncle's diner. She called to tell Shawn that her uncle was opening a new diner and he was making her a partner. Now this seventeen-year-old former prostitute was happy and half owner of her own restaurant.

Bill W.

Fulfilling your destiny allows God's plans to succeed on the earth, whether you're a mother doing her best to raise her family or a mechanic or a cook. God will take your life and make it beautiful.

One man who I feel fulfilled his destiny on earth was Bill W. Alcoholism was running rampant in his time, in the early 1900's. Alcoholics were often placed in insane asylums and received little help. Bill W. was hopelessly addicted to alcohol. After many years of misery, he finally put his alcohol problems in God's hands. This got him sober, but the problem was staying sober, which he found he could do by helping other alcoholics. That is what he did with the rest of his life, he helped other alcoholics and that was the beginning of AA. I believe AA was a move of God. It has helped millions of people all over the globe beat alcohol. But Bill W. did not know the effect his life would have on the world; he just obeyed God one step at a time.

Fulfilling our destiny will have a ripple effect across this world and the next. Even if you feel that what you are doing is unimportant it is not. God has a perfect plan.

God has a plan for your life, a perfect plan. His grace has provided for you everything you will need to fulfill that plan. You do not need to know all the details of the plan. Just follow God one step at a time, knowing that as you do His perfect plan for your life will be accomplished and your life will have mattered.

Chapter Five

Growing in Grace

But grow in the grace and knowledge of the Lord Jesus Christ. 2 Peter 3:17

We are told to grow in grace. Grace gives us the ability and the power to fulfill our purpose on earth. I want to grow in grace because I want the power and ability to do the things God has called me to do. So how do we grow in grace?

One thing we notice about the early church is they have the Holy Spirit. The Holy Spirit is poured out on them in the upper room, and this is when the book of Acts begins. Before the Holy Spirit comes, all they are doing is waiting. The Holy Spirit comes, and things start happening. Power comes. A mighty rushing wind comes roaring from heaven and fills the house where they are. Tongues of fire rest on their heads and they all begin speaking in other tongues. {Acts chapter2}

The disciples are not hiding anymore. They immediately begin preaching and that day three thousand people get saved. They begin the work they are called to do and with power and ability.

The grace they receive has a lot to do with the Holy Spirit. They are filled with the Holy Spirit, and they are obedient to Him. They go where He tells them to go, and they say what He tells them to say. I believe the Holy Spirit is key to growing in grace, because our best example of grace is the early church, and the early church is full of the Holy Spirit.

Jesus spoke a parable I believe has to do with staying filled with the Holy Spirit.

Then the kingdom of heaven shall be likened to ten virgins who took their lamps and went out to meet the bridegroom. Now five of them were wise, and five of them were foolish. Those who were foolish took their lamps and took no oil with them, but the wise took oil in the vessels with their lamps. But while the bridegroom was delayed, they all slumbered and slept. And at midnight a cry was heard; "behold the bridegroom is coming; go out and meet him!" Then all the virgins arose and trimmed their lamps. And the foolish said to the wise, "give us some of your oil for our lamps are going out." But the wise answered saying, "No lest there should not be enough for us and you; but go rather to those and buy for yourselves."

And while they went to buy, the bridegroom came,

and those who were ready went in with him to the wedding and the door was shut. Afterward the other virgins came also saying, "Lord, Lord open to us!" But he answered and said, "Assuredly I say to you I do not know you." Watch therefore, for you know neither the day nor the hour in which the Son of Man is coming. Matthew 25:1-14

This parable is about keeping ourselves full of the Holy Spirit. The Holy Spirit is the part of God that is present with us in the dispensation we are in. And since the cross of Christ, the Holy Spirit is in us and not just with us. We are to nurture a relationship with the Holy Spirit, and the Holy Spirit always points to Jesus. This had to do with the second part of our verse; *to grow in grace and the knowledge of the Lord Jesus.* The Holy Spirit gives us revelation knowledge of Jesus.

So, to grow in grace we need to keep our lamps full of oil. That means to keep ourselves filled with the Holy Spirit, He is the oil in the parable.

Now we will talk about how to keep oil in our lamps, or to keep ourselves filled with the Holy Spirit.

Focus on Jesus. The focus of our life is to be on Jesus. This will make us more alert and more sensitive to the Holy Spirit.

Be sensitive and obedient. The Holy Spirit is not a shouter, He is a whisperer. {Although when you are filled with Him you will shout!} So, we need to quiet our spirits and listen and then obey. The early church knew how to be led by Him.

Worship. I think worship is one of the very best

ways to get filled up with the Holy Spirit. That is when I feel full of Him, while I worship. The Bible also says we can just sing to ourselves and stay built up also. Keep anointed music going.

Praying in tongues. This builds us up in the Holy Spirit.

Chaste speech. Ungodly speech grieves the Holy Spirit, so don't gossip, speak negatively of others, and do not swear! Clean and beautiful speech, only, this keeps us from grieving the Holy Spirit.

Humility. We think that Jesus is humble, and He is, but the Holy Spirit is extremely humble. He has become nameless and faceless so that He might point to Christ. His voice is so quiet it can be easily passed over. We have to want to hear it. Humility will help us stay close to Him. Humility is very pleasing to God, and grace is God's favor, humility gets us more grace.

Read the Bible. Not only reading the Bible but also to listening to anointed preaching or to just meditate on a single verse or reading anointed books. All this is included.

My sister, Carol explained to me one time that reading, or hearing other people's revelations of the Word of God is feeding on the milk of the word. Because they chew it up and digest it for you. {*as newborn babes desire the pure milk of the word that you may grow thereby.1Peter2:2*} Feeding on the meat of the Word of God is getting the revelation of the Word of God for yourself. Keeping the word before you and feeding on it.

Talking about the things of God. This really works, whether it is just talking to another person or testimony time at church. {I actually haven't been to a church that does testimonies for years but when I did it was my favorite part. I got more out of it then the sermon.} Talking about God and sharing testimonies builds us up in the Holy Spirit. When my sister and I talk about the things of God together it gets us excited to be Christians, it builds us up and strengthens our faith.

Hanging out with mature Christians. If you find someone who is really full of God, try to get them to be your friend so it will rub off on you. Try to stay away from those who bring you faith down.

Be kind. Being kind, loving, tenderhearted and generous. This stuff makes the Holy Spirit happy.

Remember we want more and more of Him. This will help.

Telling others about Jesus. The Holy Spirit will lead you on what to say and to whom. Don't walk around sounding religious and turn people off. Remember also to be Christ to people. Loving and giving to those who have needs, this is the best testimony.

Now these are the same things that will help you grow in grace. Doesn't this sound a lot like the early church?

It is no big secret how to grow in grace. It is all the things we should be doing as Christians. The Holy Spirit is the key to growing in grace.

It is Not That Hard.

These things can be done and there are no limitations such as age or brains, etc. A child can grow in grace very quickly. The early church was filled with the Holy Spirit and had great grace upon them. This happened to them instantly, but then they continued to grow in grace as they stayed filled with the Holy Spirit and grew in the knowledge of the Lord Jesus Christ through Him. Remember the knowledge of the Lord Jesus Christ is revelation knowledge given by the Holy Spirit. This changes us and matures us. We become like Jesus when we see Him as He is.

Growing in grace is important and the key is the Holy Spirit, and our best example is the early church.

Chapter Six

Evidence of Grace

For the grace of God that brings salvation has appeared to all men. It teaches us to say, "No" to ungodliness and worldly passions, and to live self-controlled, upright and godly lives, in this present age, while we wait for the blessed hope- the glorious appearing of our great God and Savior, Jesus Christ, who gave Himself for us to redeem us from all wickedness and to purify Himself a people that are His very own, eager to do what is good. Titus 2:11-15

A change happens in Christians who are growing in grace. Again, we can look at the early church and see some dramatic changes in the lives of the early Christians. They have become an example, but we also can do these same things. Here are some of the signs of those who are growing in grace.

The world loses its hold over them. They detach from the things of the world, and they no longer seem important. Their possessions are no longer that important and they very willingly give them up. Many give up careers or wealth or homes to serve the Lord. It is because this world and what it has to offer does not compare to the Kingdom of Heaven which they have their eyes so firmly fixed on.

Those that have grown in grace are not living for what this world has to offer. In fact, it no longer appeals to them.

Most of us, me included, are building our own kingdom. We want to accumulate stuff. We want a house and a bank account, a car or two and lots of stuff. We want to get ahead. We want to stockpile, so we will always have enough, and we will never have to suffer. That is the next thing on the list.

Christians who have grown in grace are not afraid to suffer. Suffering loss or pain for Christ who suffered so much for us becomes more of a privilege than something to be feared. Christians who are walking in great grace will face suffering, fearlessly. It actually seems like to some it has become a joy to suffer for Christ. We will talk more about this in our chapter on suffering.

Christians who have grown in grace take joy in giving. *And remember the words of the Lord Jesus that He said, "It is more blessed to give than to receive." Acts 20:35*

I always thought that was a nice little saying, "It is more blessed to give than to receive." But I just did not believe it. I have always liked receiving better. Then one day I realized if Jesus said that it must be true. It must really be more blessed to give than to receive. This is also for the mature in grace. They are becoming more like Jesus, and they would rather give than receive.

They have greater faith.

To those mature in grace, faith increases greatly, partly because as they mature their faith is not on what they can get for their selves but how they can minister God's love to others. They are no longer living selfishly but they have lined themselves up with God's will. They will have faith working by love.

They have more gratitude.

The mature give thanks in everything because they trust God is doing what is best for them even if it looks like trouble. Many in the book of Acts were giving thanks in jail or in persecution.

They value eternal things.

Since they no longer value the things of the world, they begin to value the same things God values, which are the characteristics of Christ. They begin to look like Jesus and act like Jesus. They are storing their riches in heaven.

They are not judgmental, they value unity.

You will not hear Christians who have grown in grace gossiping. They can't gossip because they are motivated by love. They will not pass judgement on others, and they will not try to bring themselves up by putting others down because they will gladly take last place. {I am not even close to this one yet.}

They have spiritual power.

The signs that followed Jesus begin to follow them. That is healing the sick, casting out demons, raising the dead, and other supernatural miracles.

They have zeal.

You won't find people who have grown in grace sitting around playing video games; they have a lot to do. They accomplish huge things because they are following God's magnificent plan for their life.

They no longer fear men.

The Bible tells us to fear the Lord is the beginning of wisdom and the fear of man is a snare. We can see in the book of Acts the early Christians were being told to stop preaching the Good News, but they refused even though some were jailed, some were beaten, and some were killed.

These points are all evidences of those who have begun to grow in grace. The early church again is our best example, it is written about in the book of Acts. I believe we will soon begin to live like the early church again!

Chapter Seven

God Gives Grace to the Humble

But He gives us more grace. That is why scripture says: God resists the proud but gives grace to the humble. James 4:6

Satan was once Lucifer, an arc angel of great beauty. He stood before the throne of God and ministered there. Satan fell because he allowed pride to enter his heart. This was the first sin; the first turning away from God.   When Lucifer began to see his own light and beauty as coming from himself instead of God, His Creator, he turned from God and began to serve himself.   Satan fell because of his pride; therefore, God will resist the proud and He will only give His grace to the humble. Pride is actually resisting God.   Mankind has the capability of holding more of the grace of God than any other being. We have known great wickedness, and all of us have sinned, we who have been plucked out of eternal damnation through no righteousness of our own. So, we have no place for pride, only humility. We know our only righteousness comes through our faith in Jesus Christ and even that not of ourselves. Believe it or not, this gives us the potential to hold more of the power of God, because of our humble position. Our eyes are fixed on Him.

But still, most of mankind will not be saved.

Bob Jones, an incredible prophet of God, on a taped message tells of an experience in his life where his body died for a short time after an aneurism burst. While Bob was gone, he saw scenes from heaven and from hell. He stood in between the two and watched souls go to their eternal destinies. He said for everyone hundred people that had passed away only about three were making it into heaven, the other ninety-seven were descending into hell.

So why do so many choose death over life?

The answer is pride.

They cling to the same idea that Satan did, that they do not need God. They look to themselves in pride. What makes this so pitiful is in our fallen state we are the most wretched of all creation. All of our own righteousness that we cling to is only filthy rags. We truly have no reason for pride!

We hide our sin rather than come to the light and confess our sin. We shrink back in darkness and choose spiritual blindness when exposing ourselves to the Lord will set us free. At least the angels that fell were powerful majestic beings. They were not the pathetic sinful, weak creation that we have become.

Many people try to compensate for sin by good works, which they build only as a monument to themselves to detract from the sin within them. This only brings them farther from God and true righteousness which they never will find in themselves. Their works will not be able to save them no matter how noble they seem.

Others hide in religion. They religiously follow religion and take pride in their devotion to it. And they look down their noses in pride at the less diligent than they. They are even willing to kill for their religion they so zealously guard. Little do they realize there are the furthest from God, for they are the deepest in pride.

Those who are willing to come to God in humility and repentance and confess their sin are forgiven. Sometimes those who have come out of the deepest sin are the humblest. They know they were worthless and are amazed at the love of God that would rescue them. They stand in awe and gratitude at the love of God and the price of their grace. They have no pride. They have God's grace on them in abundance.

Summer Finds out She is in Pride

God told me one time that my husband Jim was very humble. At the same time, He told me that I was very proud. He told me that my husband pleased Him, and I didn't. I could not believe my ears. I prayed and read my Bible all day. I went to church every Sunday and Wednesday night. I did not do anything worldly. I never watched television or read any book that was not Christian.

My husband Jim, on the other hand was a real sinner. At the time the Lord was speaking to me Jim was sitting in the living room watching television and he had a large can of beer hiding behind the chair he was nipping on. Not only that but he had recently committed a felony and was facing prison again. This just could not be.

I could not believe all my diligent, constant time in the Bible and church wasn't impressing God, but my sinner husband was!!!

I asked Him to explain. He did. He told me that my husband was so humble before Him that anything God asked Jim to do Jim would do. Then He reminded me of many things Jim had done what God had told Him to do. Then God told me that I was rarely obedient. Then He reminded me of several things that He had told me to do, that I didn't even consider doing. {I did not want to do them; they were too hard}

Am I saying that it is alright to sin? Absolutely not! In fact, I have been trying to straighten my husband out on that for years, but for some reason God wants me to leave that to Him.

Bob Jones said something else very interesting in his taped testimony about heaven and hell that explains this.

He said, "The greater devil opposition you have down here the greater you are in heaven because you have had to fight greater wars. Some people in great leadership do not have much reward because they didn't have to fight much. But some people just coming out of carnality have great rewards."

That is my husband Jim, coming out of great carnality. Because you see Jim is not content to sin, he fights and battles sin, in fact his whole life has been an intense spiritual battle.

In the years since, I have learned a lot about humility by watching my husband Jim, I will tell you about him.

Jim sins, he can't seem to help himself sometimes, but he always repents. In fact, I can always tell when Jim has done something wrong at dinner time. Jim prays over his food at every meal. When he starts praying over his food and he has done something he is ashamed of, I will not get to eat right away. He starts praying and praying and asking God to forgive him. Jim will forget about eating.

Jim worships. He puts on worship music and sings his heart out to the Lord. Anything about his sins being forgiven especially touches Jim's heart. He has a gratitude for the Lord and what He has done for him.

Jim talks to people about the Lord. He has led a lot of people to the Lord. He considers it a privilege to tell people about the Lord.

Jim gives people stuff, not the stuff he doesn't want anymore, his favorite stuff.

I have noticed a lot of other things too. Jim always apologizes when we have a fight, even when it is my fault. I have a lot of trouble doing that. Jim doesn't have any ideas that he is too good for something; he has never been like that.

I have also noticed something else about Jim. God's heart is with Jim. His life is a testimony to the faithfulness of God.

Jesus Walked in Humility

Satan did not understand the humility of Jesus; he only saw it as weakness. Jesus the Supreme Ruler of this universe had the power to squash Satan like a bug. Not only Satan but our whole planet full of fallen sinners. But Jesus could not do that because of His great love for mankind.

Satan saw this love as weakness, in God and in Jesus. Jesus in order to save mankind entered our planet and became extremely humble and vulnerable. He was in a human body just as we are. He was infant and dependent on His mother. He had to grow up and learn like we do. He was subject to hunger and thirst and fatigue. He was still God, but He had made Himself vulnerable.

Satan could not believe his good fortune. Jesus allowed His love to make Himself vulnerable and now Satan could destroy Him.

You see, Jesus did not come to this planet in power. He came in a very lowly way. He came in love. He did not come to this planet to display His power. If He had He could have put on quite a show. He could have moved mountains or done mighty signs in the skies or anything He desired, but Jesus doesn't use power that way and for that reason.

Jesus did not come to earth to display His power. Jesus came to this earth cloaked in a human body, in weakness and humility to display His love. He proved His love by humility and suffering.

This allowed Satan to tempt Him as a human. Jesus was hungry and thirsty in the wilderness, and subject to great temptation from Satan. But Jesus persevered. Then Satan tortured and killed Jesus and Jesus in humility and loved surrendered to unbelievable suffering. Satan did not see this as strength but as weakness.

Satan understands pride and a great show of his power and beating his constituents in to fearful submission. This is his idea of power and strength. He thought he could beat Jesus in this way.

Jesus came in great humility and love. He endured incredible suffering in humility because of that love. This is true strength. Those with this kind of strength can be entrusted with a greater grace. Those with this kind of strength can be trusted with God's power, because God gives His power to be used in love. Jesus became low but He ascended on high. He reached the very lowest depth there was, and He ascended to the greatest position, there is no higher. But this was accomplished through love and humility. He has become our example.

For this reason, *God resists the proud, but gives grace to the humble.*

Chapter Eight

Grace for Suffering

Looking unto Jesus, the author and finisher of our faith, who for the joy that was set before Him endured the cross, despising the shame, and has sat down at the right hand of the throne of God. Hebrews 12:2

Those who grow in grace begin to look at suffering differently. One example of this is Apostle Paul in the book of Acts. As Paul was heading to Jerusalem he stopped and stayed in Caesarea. While he was there Agabus, the prophet, came and took Paul's belt and bound his own hands and feet. Then he prophesied that the owner of the belt would so be bound by the Jews and handed over to the Gentiles in Jerusalem. {Acts 21} Even though Paul was warned he went to Jerusalem anyway. There He was arrested and bound, and he was imprisoned.

For a long time, I could never understand why Paul did not turn around and head the other direction. He was warned that there was suffering ahead, and he still went. I certainly do not enjoy suffering and would have not gone to Jerusalem. But Paul went on purpose, knowing what was coming and he suffered. My mind couldn't comprehend that because suffering was to be avoided at all costs in my line of thinking.

I think I am beginning to understand now, though. Paul went for the same reason that Jesus went to the cross. This was God's plan for Paul's life. God actually puts suffering in His plans! He did for Jesus and He did for Paul. But Paul had a choice. He did not have to suffer, he was warned. He chose to suffer.

Do you find this as incredible as I do? Paul chose the best way. He chose a path much like the Lord's path. He chose a narrower path, and he chose a higher calling. He chose the path which was the hardest but would take him the farthest.

This is something so precious to God, when men on earth, willing choose to suffer for Him. Let's look at this.

We are living on this terrestrial ball, called earth, which is the only place that the glory of God is veiled. We see God only very dimly through the eyes of faith. Our planet is covered with a thick veil of unbelief and darkness coming from the evil one, Satan. He wants us to believe that nothing matters, and we are to do as we please with our short little time on earth. The whole of humanity is rushing downward in a river of complacency that naturally flows away from God. This false reality contains many cleverly crafted lies that people believe to cloak them from the truth of their spiritual state; which is fallen.

When a person chooses to serve God, we choose to follow the unseen. We have to walk by faith, not sight. We turn from everything we know and start paddling up stream against the current the rest of the world is floating down. We face the light instead of fleeing from it which begins an uncomfortable process that exposes the many layers of sin in our hearts. We begin to follow a tiny little voice in our spirit that we can barely hear; often times wondering if it is God or our imagination. We leave the broad and easy path and begin to follow a difficult and narrow path. We seem foolish to the world that sees us paddling upstream, they don't understand our devotion to Christ who appeals to us more than the pleasures of this world.

Jesus forged this path we now follow. He forged it through His life on earth. He walked in humility, love and suffering. He was not here on a pleasure trip.

He is light in the darkness. He is the Way, the Truth and the Life, in a world full of darkness and lies. No one understood Him on earth, not His family or His friends or even His disciples, because He was building an unseen kingdom. He was living a life that did not make sense to mortal minds. He did things like not eat for forty days and nights, and like speak the truth when the truth was unpopular. He loved His enemies, and He loved the unacceptable. Yes, He died on the cross, the ultimate sacrifice, but He lived every day of His life in death to the world and alive to God.

When humans on earth, in such darkness, choose to walk the same path as Christ, forsaking the world as

Christ did, then we prove ourselves worthy of the high calling of Christ.

We do not know what this means, and we won't in this lifetime. It has to do with a world which is yet to come. It has to do with power and authority and becoming kings and priests. It has to do with having more power than angels, but becoming worthy to hold that power, by becoming conformed to the image of Christ.

Paul understood about suffering, instead of turning around at Caesarea, he went on to Jerusalem. He willingly chose to suffer. Paul chose a similar path to Christs.

This increased his measure of grace.

It is precious to God when humans willingly choose to suffer.

Jesus Learns the Beauty of Suffering

Have you ever wondered how Jesus endured His extreme suffering? The Bible tells us it was for the joy that was set before Him. My daughter, Joy was given a revelation how Jesus was prepared for suffering as a boy.

Joy saw Jesus as young boy watching his mother give birth. He was near her and watching as her pains increased. He was moved by such compassion watching His mother going through deep anguish and pain that He wanted to heal her. But the Holy Spirit refrained Him and told Him to just watch.

Jesus did and when his mother had given birth, Jesus saw her anguish turn to joy as she took the new baby into her arms. The Holy Spirit was preparing Jesus how to endure His own suffering. He endured, remembering His mother's labor and remembering the joy that followed as a new birth took place.

We are the birth that brought Jesus so much joy, which enabled Him to endure such immense suffering. We, the children of God, bring our Savior intense joy. He has birthed us. The thought of us gave Him the joy to endure the cross.

So great was this lesson to Jesus that He taught it to His disciples before their time of suffering. They had left all to follow Jesus, and He had become the most important thing to them, and they were about to have Him ripped away from them. Jesus was preparing them for suffering.

"Most assuredly, I say to you that you will weep and lament, but the world will rejoice; and you will be sorrowful, but your sorrow will be turned to joy. A woman, when she is in labor, has sorrow because her time has come; but soon as she has given birth to the child, she no longer remembers the anguish, for joy that a human being has been born into the world. Therefore, you now have sorrow; but I will see you again and your heart will rejoice, and your joy no one will take from you." John 16:20-22

Joy follows suffering. Grace is present during suffering.

Grace for Suffering

We will have times of suffering, but God gives us grace to get through those times of suffering. But to those who chose to suffer for Christ, they will increase greatly in grace. Many Christians have chosen to suffer for Christ through the ages and some have even laid down their lives.

I want to quote for you a passage from the book, *Jesus Freaks,* by dc Talk. It is a book about martyrs. This passage is about Thomas Hauker, a believer from England who was martyred in 1555.

"Thomas," his friend lowered his voice so as not to be heard by the guard. 'I have to ask you this favor. I need to know if what the others say about the grace of God is true. Tomorrow, when they burn you at the stake, if the pain is tolerable and your mind is still at peace, lift your hands above your head. Do it right before you die. Thomas, I have to know.

Thomas Hauker whispered to his friend, "I will."

The next morning Hauker was bound at the stake and the fire was lit. The fire burned a long time, but Hauker was motionless. His skin was burnt to a crisp and his fingers were gone. Everyone watching supposed he was dead. Suddenly, miraculously, Hauker lifted his hands, still on fire, over his head. He reached them up to the living God, and then with great rejoicing, clapped them together three times.

The people there broke into great rejoicing and applause. Hauker's friend had his answer.

This man Hauker was experiencing joy in his suffering. This was great grace at work in his life. Those who choose to suffer for Christ enter a level of grace and joy that carries them through to a new level in God. They become like Christ.

Like Paul we also can chose a narrow path that looks like the one Jesus took, we can choose to suffer for His sake.

Chapter Nine

God's Strength Made Perfect in Weakness

To keep me from becoming conceited because of these surpassingly great revelations, there was given me a thorn in my flesh, a messenger of Satan, to torment me. Three times I pleaded with the Lord to take it away from me. But He said to me, "My grace is sufficient for you, for my power is made perfect in weakness." Therefore, I will boast all the more gladly about my weaknesses, so that Christ's power may rest on me. That is why for Christ's sake. I delight in weaknesses, in insults, in hardships, in persecutions, in difficulties. For when I am weak, then I am strong. 2 Corinthians 12:7-10

Remember in my introduction, when I said my husband and I have lived a life of grace. We have lived a life of grace because of our weakness. God has been our only hope. We know what it is to be at the bottom of the barrel. Do you know what it is like to have everyone think you are worthless and treat you accordingly, and soon you believe it yourself? {Many of you do.} Do you know what it is like to be under the authority of someone who despises you and can squash you like a bug, and that is their plan? My husband and I do. That was our life.

When I met my husband, he was twenty-seven, almost twenty eight and I had just turns seventeen. He had been incarcerated, in one form or another, much of his childhood and pretty much all of his adult life. He had just gotten out of prison for the second time, the first time he had violated parole and was sent back again. To say he was wild would be putting it mildly. He was classified in prison as the highest risk and kept only in maximum security. The rare times that Jim wasn't locked up he lived in Detroit, and he was known by the police department there very well.

Jim had to transfer his parole to move to where I lived, a much smaller town. His new parole officer was Mr. Long. Mr. Long did not want him here and hated him immediately. He was considered big time trouble and they, the justice system in our town, were looking to lock him up again. This is how the world saw him. I saw him differently.

I was empty on the inside. I was a Christian, yes, but my personality was nonexistent. I was a good pretender. I had a big empty hole inside me where a person should have been. I had no feelings, except fear. I didn't like life. I had no plans or dreams. I copied other people's personalities to make up for the lack of my own. There really wasn't anything that I wanted until Jim came along.

  Jim was sunshine in a world of darkness. Jim has acquired something in his life of pain, it is warmth. He radiates warmth. I was instantly attracted. I was attracted to the warmth.

  I wasn't the only one who felt his warmth. Jim also attracts children and animals. He seems to have a little magic. They are just drawn to him.

  Through the years Jim has had many of his own animals, always strays that just showed up at our house and adopted Jim. But even the neighbor's dogs would prefer Jim to their own masters. One time we had next door neighbors that had a huge German Shepherd in their fenced yard. If their dog got out of the fence, they would have to chase him because he never would come for them. Many times, I saw them running for blocks trying to catch him. But if Jim were around all he had to do was whistle and that dog would come running. That dog loved Jim. Other dogs around did the same thing.

  One time a doctor lived down the street from us. His dog would stay at our house every night until the middle of the night before it would go home. It wanted to be near Jim.

  And little children are drawn to him too. As I look back through our scrap books, I noticed this again. Whenever a child around our house was in tears they usually ended up on Jim's lap for comfort. Not just our own children but others as well. The scrap book is filled with children on Jim's lap with little tear stained faces.

  In fact, not too long ago a friend came over,

who is raising a tiny little girl who had been taken from her mother by the human services department in our area. This little girl was so darling I just wanted to hold her, but I could not get near her, she clutched my friend in fear. But soon she was in Jim's arms and there she stayed. This little girl still won't come to me, she is too shy, but every time they come over, she toddles back to Jim and crawls up on his lap.

But Jim's magic seems to even go past just children and animals, to those who are hurting. I remember one time when we were in a big city. I wasn't used to big cities and they scare me. We came around the corner of a building and there was a line of bums sitting against the wall. Jim did not shrink back like the rest of us that were with him. That special light that is inside Jim turned on as he walked down the row of bums and shook each one's hand. One old man smiled from ear to ear a big old toothless grin. Jim can bring smiles out of people.

My sister, Carol, tears up when she talks about Jim. She has felt his warmth. I have heard her say, "He is the kindest person I've ever met."

Carol had trouble a few years back. She had almost like a nervous breakdown. She went through a rough spell, and no one seemed to understand what she was going through, me included. Her family didn't understand either. She told me later that Jim was the only one that seemed to understand. I would be at work, but Jim was home during the day. She would come over and just sit. Jim told her to. Jim understands pain.

When I met Jim at seventeen years old, even

though he was very handsome, it was his warmth that attracted me. I felt like sleeping beauty. He climbed into the cold thorn covered tower that held my sleeping heart and woke up my feelings with a kiss. But it wasn't me he kissed; he kissed my doll, Snooks.

Even though I was seventeen years old I still held my doll, whenever I wasn't at school. I slept with her every night. I had my whole life. Even though I was seventeen I played with my doll, all the time, she was my world. Jim entered my world when he asked to see my doll and he kissed her.

I was so attracted; all I wanted was to be with him. I wanted to be with him every second of every day. I could not help myself. Suddenly I wanted something, and it was all I wanted. I wanted to be a wife. I wanted to be Jim's wife. But I was so void on the inside and ashamed of me, that I could not say that to anyone, not even myself. I just followed him around. I was happy when I was with him. I was happy doing nothing, just sitting with him, being near him. I needed him.

We were two nobodies. We were super nobodies. Even though we were both Christians and loved the Lord we were two broken people. Jim could not stay out of trouble. He had been in trouble his whole life and he continued to get in trouble.

His parole officer Mr. Long decided they were going to send him away for a long time. He told me so. He said I probably wouldn't see him again for at least six years.

I cannot tell you how scary it is for me to sit

in a courthouse, waiting to find out what is going to happen to my whole world. This wasn't the last time. I had many, many times to come.

I would be sitting there full of fear, my whole life in the balance. All I want is one thing, my husband and I to be together and raise our three children, and it seems to be all up to these people in this courthouse. I feel like human garbage as these well-dressed people walk in and out laughing like nothing is happening.

It was like facing a firing squad. In fact, facing a firing squad would have been easier. It wasn't dying that scared me, it was living, and I couldn't live without Jim.

After the horrible waiting, the worst part was when would stand before the judge. They usually would talk to him as if he was worthless, and the truth was, he was always guilty of what he was up there for. Jim has always pled guilty every time he has been to court, because he has always been guilty.

My husband has actually been arrested so many times since I have known him, I can't remember them all, I am going to guess maybe nine or ten times.

But I can remember the feeling of sitting in the courthouse, sometimes alone, sometimes with small children and then we would have to wait out in the hall. And always, I would pray the same prayer because I felt so, so, so worthless. Lord, please someday, somewhere let someone see that Jim is good.

He was good, he took care of us, his wife and three children the best he could. But he was broken, and I was broken. We did not have a chance in this world.

I hated the way the judges would talk to Jim. I hated standing before judges; there was nothing I feared more.

But this is not the end to this story because something happened so wonderful and so amazing that even though it is my life and it happened to me; it still seems impossible. God gave us a life. We could not do it on our own; in our weakness He has been strong. Over and over God has saved our family.

Jim did not go to prison for six years like Mr. Long said. The charges were dropped, and Jim only served seven months for a parole violation. Soon after Jim got home from that stretch we got married. That was the last time Jim did time in prison. God gave me a promise when I married Jim that Jim would not go back to prison.

Jim has not gone back but he has faced it over and over again and God had given us miracle after miracle. I have been told many times by officials I would not see my husband for years. God had other plans.

You see there is something so real and so strong and so powerful in this world that even the hopeless have hope and that is God's GRACE!

Jim and I have been carried through the years by God's grace from one disaster after another. We have been through a lot.

Alcoholism

Poverty

Depression

Sicknesses

Danger

Spiritual Battles

Mental illness

I wrote more about it in my book *The Impossible Marriage,* but in all our troubles and weaknesses we have seen God's grace in miraculous ways. That is because we needed miracles, we could not survive without them.

God's grace was made perfect in our weakness. He has filled in every crack and crevice of our brokenness with his marvelous wonderful grace.

Jim and I just recently celebrated our thirty sixth wedding anniversary this year. We are still here, and we are still serving God. You see it is true, it is really true, God's strength is made perfect in weakness. We have made it here by grace.

Chapter Ten

Special Grace

The law was added so that the trespass might increase. But where sin increased grace increased all the more, so that just as sin reigned in death, so also grace might reign through righteousness to bring eternal life through Jesus Christ our Lord. Romans 5:20

There are places and times when God's grace increases. God's heart is so moved by the needs of mankind that in great need; His grace increases. That is what I am calling special grace.

Prisons

One area of special grace is prisons. Prisons are the junkyard of society. This is where we throw away humans. I know it has to be because we can't have murderers and rapists running the streets and I am all for prisons. But God's special grace hovers over prisons and jail cells. God is near because of the suffering and the brokenness. Those in prison who call out to Him will receive His grace in abundance. They need it. And many have found God's grace there. Not only is God's grace poured out on prisons, God takes it personally when someone helps those in prison. It is also like helping Him. He will thank us personally.

Orphanages

God's grace is also especially on orphanages. His heart is moved by children and especially by orphans. Children without parents are in the most vulnerable position they could be in. God is always especially moved by the weak.

Pure and undefiled religion before God and the Father is this: to visit orphans and widows in their trouble, and to keep oneself unspotted by the world. James 1:27

A father of the fatherless, a defender of widows, Is God in His holy habitation. Psalm 68:5

The Lord watches over strangers; He relieves the fatherless and the widow. Psalm 146:9

God's huge heart is so moved by orphans to help them is to help Him. He hears the cry of the fatherless.

Do you remember in chapter two, when I told you about my sister Carol and I being fatherless? God heard the cry of our tiny hearts. Although we never were able to verbalize our terror to adults, our inner cries were heard by God. There was a very happy ending for us, and I know that I know, it was the hand of God.

One day when we were still quite small my mother brought home a new boyfriend. He seemed to pay as much attention to Carol and I as he did to our mom. Mom may have been smitten but Carol and I were really smitten. He not only married our mom he adopted two little girls. Carol and I had a real dad, and now we had a stay at home mom.

We have never gotten over the relief we felt on our parents wedding day. We knew our nightmare was over and it was.

We still feel the relief all these years later. My sister, Carol, goes to great lengths to get dad the right Father's Day card every year. She stands at the card shop and reads every card, and she stands there and cries as she reads each one.

Every year on Father's Day we try to convey to our dad just how much he means to us, but I just don't think he will really ever know. But God knows, because it was His special grace that brought him to us.

The Sick

Although Jesus paid for our healing on the cross, not everyone is healed. I can't give you a reason for this except to tell you God's grace is on the sick in a special way. He never takes our suffering lightly. No matter how much we suffer we can still trust Him knowing He is near, and His heart is moved by our call.

I have been healed by God, many many times, but the last five years I have had six surgeries and one for cancer. I have been healed at times and I have had to go to the doctor's and seek medical help other times, but God's grace has always been present.

Again, God counts it as a personal favor when we help the sick. His heart is near to the sick.

The Homeless

The homeless also have a special grace. God is closer to those who are in a rough spot and the homeless are in a rough spot. Many people are homeless because of drug addiction, mental illness or alcoholism. But also, many are homeless because they have no one to fall back on in an emergency. It can happen to anyone. Whatever the reason the homeless are special to God. He is with them and His big heart is moved.

There are many other situations where God's special grace is present. These are just a few. Anywhere that someone is suffering, and mistreated, God's special grace abounds.

God is so in tune with suffering people that He actually takes on their identity. This is special grace!

What do I mean that He takes on their identity? Their problem becomes His problem. He is there and His compassion is aroused. We find this in scripture.

Then the righteous will answer Him, saying," Lord when have we seen You hungry and have fed you, or thirsty and have given You drink? And when have we seen You a stranger and taken You in, or naked and have clothed You? And when have we seen You sick or in prison and have come to You?"

And the king will answer and say to them, "Truly I say to you, Inasmuch as you have done it to one of these, the least of My brothers you have done it to Me." Matthew 25:37-40

God's special grace is so upon those in need that to help them is to literally help God. God is near and dear to the broken hearted and those in humble circumstances.

His grace hovers in here, He is closer, He is present. This is special grace.

Chapter Eleven

Those Who Fall Through the Cracks

Do not rejoice over me, my enemy;
When I fall, I will arise;
When I sit in darkness,
The Lord will be a light to me. Micah 7:8

Dear Brother or Sister in Christ,

I have something I want to say because it is burning in my heart. This message comes out in some form or another in every book I write because it is one of the biggest lessons I have learned in my life, and it has taken my whole life to learn it. I have learned what I am about to say from being married to Jim.

I have seen Jim struggle with sin our whole marriage. He is an alcoholic, he has also struggled with drug addiction, and he has had trouble with about every sin there is. Jim really hates it when I write this stuff because he is sure everyone will hate him. I hope you will not hate him. But I know there are other Christians who struggle with sin and can't seem to get free and that is why I am putting Jim through this again.

There are those who seem like failures in this life. They struggle with something, like Jim, and they don't seem to get anywhere. They certainly don't fit in to the role model of a Christian. In fact, some people won't even try to live the Christian life because they know they can't do it. They know their sin is bigger than they are. I want to give them hope.

Jim wanted to live a Christian life, but he failed a lot. I know there are others like him. To the rest of us they seem to be backslidden and we let them know, they better repent. Believe me Jim has heard this from everyone including me.

I did not realize when I first married Jim, the extent of Jim's problems. I thought I knew, but I didn't. After a year or so I started to get the picture, that in order to face life on a daily basis Jim was using something, alcohol or drugs, and that wasn't all he did wrong!

I realized Jim was quite the sinner! So, I knew he must not really be saved. I had to do something about this. I couldn't let the man I love go to hell. I decided to pray for him.

So, I prayed. I prayed diligently. I prayed without ceasing. I prayed my every waking moment. I was not going to give God a break until Jim was saved; I just loved

Jim too much. "God save Jim, God save Jim, God save Jim, God save Jim!"

After a couple of weeks God had enough. I heard Him audibly. His booming voice sounded a little miffed, "He already IS SAVED!"

"Oh."

Jim did not seem to think he was saved, even though he loved the Lord, even though he went to church every Sunday, even though he prayed and read his Bible. He knew he was a sinner. Jim would try over and over to get saved. Every time we went to a meeting where no one knew him, and it came time for the salvation invitation. You know the routine.

"Every head bowed and every eye closed. If you have never asked Jesus to be your Lord and Savior raise your hand now."

Up would go Jim's hand.

Or some places you would have to go down to the altar.

There he would go.

Sometimes he would get baptized, again and again.

Many times, he would go forward for prayer for deliverance from alcohol. I have seen this one over and over again also. Jim would go forward to repent for his drinking and ask for prayer. I have been up there with him and have heard this so many times I can't count.

"I used to have a problem with alcohol, too," they would tell him.

Jim's eyes would light up with hope. Maybe they could tell him how to get free.

"God just delivered me."

I have heard that said to Jim so many times and I would see the hope drain out of his face, because God did not deliver Jim.

Jim has tried and failed and tried and failed and tried and failed.

Oh, a couple of times I heard them tell him this one, "God forgives you, just don't do it again."

Jim would leave broken hearted. But he kept trying.

Jim has checked himself into rehab nine times. Sometimes he would be gone for months. He had a wife and three kids to support, so that was not easy. In addition to his nine times in rehab he has been in county jails five or six times too, that is another kind of rehab.

I also wondered why God wasn't doing for Jim, what he had done for all these countless other people.

God told me one time after a short reprieve from Jim's drinking, "There is going to be no miracle for Jim to stop drinking. He will get a little stronger and a little stronger and the drinking will get less and less."

What God did not tell me that day was it would take a lifetime. Jim is in his sixties now, and yes, he is sober most of the time, but he still has slips.

Some people don't get miracles! Some people do not fit into our role model of a Christian. Jim certainly did not fit into mine! He did not even fit into his own. Yes, Jim still slips his hand up at altar calls and he just got baptized again about a year ago.

I know there are other people like Jim. They feel

they have fallen through the cracks of life.

Some people are sick, and they don't get healed. Everyone else gets healed, but they don't get healed. Is it their fault? Is something wrong with their faith? Is something wrong with Jim's faith?

God has told me something about this sinner husband of mine. I have tried and tried to tell this to Jim, but he just doesn't believe me.

God is very pleased with Jim.

God has spoken to me about Jim with emotion in His voice, because Jim moves God to emotion. God told me, "Jim won't quit trying. He sees his own sin and thinks he will never make it, but still, he won't give up. He thinks maybe there is a chance I will make it to heaven, and he just won't quit trying."

It is no small thing to move God to emotion. Jim has.

God also told me that Jim has a much higher place in heaven than I do. God even let me see into the future. I got to see Jim in heaven, actually a couple of times. Even though it hasn't happened yet, I got to see Jim when Jesus presents him to the Father.

I think God showed me that because I have spent my whole life praying for Jim and he will not be totally whole until that moment. It was so beautiful to see, because even standing there next Jesus, Jim was afraid to lift his head. He was afraid to face the Father. It was a holy moment when he looked up and saw he was accepted, then God drew Jim into Himself and I could not see him anymore. That will be his miracle healing, in that moment.

Some people fall through the cracks in this life. But what we don't see is God has no cracks. That is what grace does. It seals every crack.

I remember back when I was in my teens and my parents had a prison ministry. There was man in prison named Clarence.

He was a Christian and he wrote beautiful letters to many of the people at our church. Clarence was doing a lengthy prison sentence but as the years went by, he kept up his fellowship with the Christians at church and everyone was excited when he finally got out. He seemed to have grown so much as a Christian through the years that we all had such high hopes for him.

I was married and, in my twenties, when Clarence finally got out. Soon I heard that Clarence had not made it and was back in prison with another lengthy prison sentence.

I felt heartbroken for Clarence. I realized that he was not going to get out again for many years. His life seemed to me, to be ruined. In my mind it seemed like the end for Clarence.

As I was praying for Clarence, God showed me that some people will never get what they need here on earth. {I was still young at this point and even though I believed in heaven, it did not seem real to me.} Some people wouldn't ever make it in this world, like Clarence. But God let me know Clarence would be totally fulfilled in heaven. There was going to be a happy ending to Clarence's story. It was just coming in another world.

If you have fallen through the cracks in this life, I

hope you know that I am writing to you. If you feel you are too bad for God, or you are wondering why you just can't be like these other Christians, or it seems you will never make it for any reason at all. I want you to know, it is not over yet.

If your life has just been one big struggle and it seems like all you do is fail, please don't count yourself out. As imperfect as you are, you are covered by grace; you are perfect in His sight.

You will never know in this lifetime how incredible it is that you keep trying. Don't give up. Struggle, go ahead, and try again. If you can just hold onto that tiny bit of hope and keep trying. You may be in a prison cell, or sick or you may feel that no one in this world cares about you or knows you exist. You also may feel your life is hopeless and will never work.

But there is something that you cannot see, God is watching you. Your struggles are precious to Him. When you refuse to stop trying, His huge heart is moved. When you fall again and again, He is not disappointed because He knows what you are up against.

You may see yourself as too broken to be fixed, just too weak and a failure. What you don't realize is every time you try again you get stronger, and stronger. You may see a failure, but God sees a champion. Do not compare yourself to others who do not have the struggles you have. Just take another step and another step closer to God.

Remember that God sees differently than people see. I looked at my husband and saw a sinner; but not

God, God has chosen a higher place in heaven for him than for me. I haven't been through what he has been through. He feels like a failure, but he is not. He won't stop trying.

You have not lost the battle if you haven't quit fighting. You are still in the race. Your finish line may be in this life, or it may be in the next. For some it is in the next.

You are not running this race alone. All of heaven is watching you. They take notice when God is moved. And when you get back up again, He notices. Then when you refuse to stay down, God stands also. This causes all of heaven to cheer.

You see God is moved by the humble, and the lowly heart, the heart that struggles to live for Him. You are a priority to Him. Things look different in heaven, nobodies are somebodies. The invisible are visible. Those who have fallen through the cracks are priorities and the worthless are those who have great value.

If you have given up on yourself, I want you to try again. You are not alone. It is not over. There is a finish line for you, it may be on earth, or it may be in heaven. You do not have to look like other Christians look. Just don't give up. Just keep trying. Believe me in God's way of doing things you won't fall through the cracks. His grace has sealed up the cracks. Don't give up.

Love, Your sister in Christ, Summer

Chapter Twelve

Once Saved Always Saved?

We are not to take God's grace lightly. A huge price was paid for our grace as we discussed in another chapter. In fact, there was no higher price that could have been paid. The highest price has been paid. Jesus gave us His all and He is still giving us His all. He has given all He has to give. Grace is so holy and so precious, and we are to treat it as such. But there are those who treat it lightly. It happened in the early church, and it had to do with communion.

Communion

On that awful night just before Jesus began to carry that hideous load of sin, He took bread and broke it.

And He took bread, gave thanks and broke it saying, "This is My body which is given for you; do this in remembrance of Me."Likewise He also took the cup after supper saying, "This cup is the new covenant in my blood, which is shed for you." Luke 22:19-29

Communion is to remind us of the high price of grace. Communion is a powerful act. Many are healed taking communion. I know communion is very important to God. I found this out when my little girl was two years old.

My children were very young when they came to the Lord. My son, Jamie was three. It was huge to him even though he was only three. He immediately became an evangelist and told everyone he saw about Jesus. Then my next child, Lonna, was also three, when she came to the Lord. She insisted on being baptized and was baptized on a Sunday evening before the whole church. Jamie also decided to be baptized that same day.

Then when my third child, Joy came along, Jamie was six and Lonna was almost four. They could not wait until Joy was old enough to talk, so they could lead her to the Lord. By the time Joy was two she had been led to the Lord multiple times by her older brother and sister.

About the time Joy turned two, we came back to Michigan, from Florida for a period of four months, so we were going to church up here. The church we went to at this time did communion monthly.

At communion time the pastor gave a talk that we each should search our hearts before taking communion, and then he added we should not let our small children take it. So, in obedience to the Pastor when the elements came by, I did not let Joy, who was two years old, take communion.

The next month the same thing happened, only this time as the elements came around the Lord spoke to me almost audibly, "You obeyed man last month, this month obey Me. Joy is to have communion."

Of course, I obeyed. But I realized how important this must be. God was determined this tiny believer received it.

Something powerful happens when we take communion. It is to be revered and taken remembering the huge price paid for us.

The early church forgot this. Paul wrote in Corinthians and rebuked them.

Therefore, when you come together in one place, it is not to eat the Lord's Supper. For in eating one takes his own supper ahead of others; and one is hungry, and another is drunk. What! Do you not have houses to eat and drink in? Or do you despise the church and shame those who have nothing? What shall I say to you? Shall I praise you in this? I do not praise you.

For I received from the Lord that which I also delivered to you: that the Lord Jesus on the same night in which he was betrayed took bread; and when He had given thanks, He broke it and said, "This is My body which is broken for you; do this in remembrance of Me." In the same manner He also took the cup after supper, saying, "This cup is the new covenant in My blood. This do, as often as you drink it, in remembrance of Me."

For as often as you eat this bread and drink this cup, you proclaim the Lord's death til He comes. Therefore, whoever eats this bread and drinks this cup in an unworthy manner will be guilty of the body and the blood of Lord. But let a man examine himself, and so let him eat of the bread and drink of the cup. For he who eats and drinks in an unworthy manner eats and drinks judgement to himself, not discerning the Lord's body. For this reason, many are weak and sick among you, and many sleep. 1 Corinthians 11:20-30 NKJ

These people treated lightly, something very holy. I don't think they were bad, but they just forgot what was important. But what happened was many of them were sick and some of them had died! This is serious stuff here! They did not revere the death and resurrection of Christ in communion. We are not to treat this lightly!

God's grace is also a holy gift and is to be treated as such. This means taking seriously the act of communion, but this also shows us the attitude we are to have about the price of grace.

I am writing all this to make a very important point, probably one of the most important points in this book, because something worse than taking communion lightly is happening in the church today. Many in the church are condoning willful sin because of grace.

God's grace is not a license to sin!!!!!!!!
WE CAN'T DO THIS!!!!!!!!!!!!!!!!!!!!!!!!!!!!

This is not what grace is for. Grace covers our sin, YES. And that is because God has reached out to the sinner and the broken. He covers us with His grace while He picks up the shattered pieces of our soul and gently and delicately puts us back together. He will not ask us to do what we are not strong enough to do. He will push us and stretch us past what we think we can do, but He will not set us up for failure by requiring us to do what we are not strong enough to do.

His grace covers us and makes us perfect in His sight until His work in us finished. There are those who look like first class sinners who are more righteous than you because they are putting more effort into their Christian walk than you are. Remember God sees hearts! He knows the damage that has been done to each soul and He treats them accordingly.

But there are many in the churches today who believe that grace means you can willfully sin. I heard an evangelist on television, who travels from church to church talk about this. He told how after the service, one pastor told him, "See those girls in the front row. You pick out the one you want, and I will send her to your motel room."

What!!!???

Grace does not cover this!

At another church he said there was a meeting in the basement after the service. It was for wife swapping. These churches are teaching you are under grace, you can do this stuff!

What!!???

They are treating something holy with no respect. It is profane! Grace will not cover this either!!!

There is a church in our town teaching that God will never let you suffer, in fact, Jesus death wasn't even necessary.

What???!!!

People, we are to take up our cross and follow the Lord! There is going to be suffering. This is crazy!! I believe this is why the Lord asked me to write this book. This has to stop!

WE cannot treat grace with disrespect!!!!! In the early church those who took communion disrespectfully died! We cannot do worse by committing any sin and expecting grace to cover us!!! No! No! No!

"Once Saved Always Saved?"

"Once saved always saved" is the name of a doctrine that has been floating around the church for quite some time. The doctrine believes that once you are saved you can never lose your salvation. This is the doctrine behind these mega sinners in the church today that are doing this super sinning.

I think my answer to this question "Once save always saved?" is going to surprise you. My answer to this is, "No and Yes". My first answer is "NO" to once save always saved because it is possible to lose your salvation, although it is hard. God makes it easy to get in and hard to get out. Let's start with scripture.

No

For it is impossible for those who were once enlightened, and have tasted the heavenly gift, and have become partakers of the Holy Spirit, and have tasted the good word of God and the powers of the age to come, if they fall away, to renew them again to repentance, since they crucify again for themselves the Son of God, and put Him to open shame. Hebrews6:4-6

In this scripture it says that this person has lost their salvation and cannot repent again. But this cannot happen to just any Christian this is a very mature Christian. There are 5 levels of maturity they have attained and then they openly deny Christ.

The five levels are 1. They are enlightened   2. They have tasted the heavenly gift. 3. They are a partaker of the Holy Spirit 4. They have tasted the good word, 5. They have the powers of the age to come. This is a very mature Christian and they have publicly denied Christ. This is very rare. Most everyone can repent. My reason for sharing this scripture though is to show that it is possible to lose your salvation. I want to share a couple more.

Brethren, if anyone among you wanders from the truth, and someone turns him back, let him know that he who turns a sinner away from error of his way will save a soul from death and cover a multitude of sins James 5:19-20

So wandering from the truth can also lead to death spiritually. I want to quote one more and this is for those who think they can commit any sin and be right with God.

> *For if we sin willfully after we have received the knowledge of the truth, there no longer remains a sacrifice for sins, but a certain fearful expectation of judgement, and fiery indignation which will devour the adversaries. Anyone who has rejected Moses 'law dies without mercy on the testimony of two or three witnesses, of how much worse punishment, do you suppose, will he be thought worthy who has trampled the Son of God underfoot, counted the blood of the covenant by which he was sanctified a common thing, and insulted the Spirit of grace? Hebrews 10:26-29*

We cannot treat the sacrifice of Jesus as a license to sin. It is to be treated with holiness and reverent awe.

So, my first answer to once saved always saved is, No.

Yes

Now I want to give my "Yes" answer to "Once saved always saved."

If you love God and are trying; it is impossible for you to lose your salvation. You cannot lose it. Your salvation depends on His righteousness and not your own. He has taken care of all your failures. His blood will cover you until you are made perfect, and you will be made perfect. Now I will give you scripture for this.

> *All that the Father gives Me will come to Me, and*

the one who comes to Me I will by no means cast out. John 6:37

And I will give them eternal life, and they shall never perish; neither shall anyone snatch them out of My hand. John 10:28

being confident of this very thing that He who has begun a good work in you will complete it until the day of Jesus Christ; Philippians 1:6

If we confess our sins, He is faithful and just to forgive our sins and to cleanse us from all unrighteousness 1 John 1:9

There are those who don't think they can ever be right with God, so they don't even try. They look at church people and they know they can never be like that. So, they give up. They know they can never get out of the sin they are in because it is all they know.

If that is you, then I want to tell you, you don't have to be like church people. That is what grace is all about! God wants you just the way you are. He will lead you gently one step at a time just be obedient to Him. Am I giving a license to sin, absolutely not. But God will never require of someone what He knows they cannot do. He does not set people up for failure.

God Wasn't Angry with Me

Several years back when we first bought the house we are living in now, I was worried about being able to keep up financially. Buying this house was a huge spiritual victory over the enemy, but now I was getting pummeled. I went from the mountain top to the valley, quick.

Our house needed huge repairs and the mortgage was double that of the home we had just moved from. To make matters worse my husband was fired from his job [again]. I was angry with him this time. I just wanted to blame him, and I was. I flipped out. I was in extreme hysterics. Crying and screaming for hours and I put him into the same mode. It was bad, it was really bad. This all happened on Good Friday.

On Good Friday our church has open communion for three hours from noon to three o'clock. It is an absolutely beautiful time. You quietly go in and sit down in the pews. There is worship music playing and you can sit and pray as long as you like. When you are ready you can go up to the front and take communion. This was the neatest part. There is a table up front that was set up like the last supper. It has a head chair set for Jesus at the center of the table and in His spot was a beautiful prayer shawl draped up over His chair. Then there were twelve chairs set around a beautifully set table and twelve glasses of grape juice and plates of bread, set out for the communion. Every year this was a holy moment for me. It felt like I was literally sitting down at the table with the Lord.

Jim and I wanted to go to communion this day but every time we started to leave the fighting would start again. I was so angry with him.

Finally, just before three o'clock we managed to get in the car and drive to the church. I managed to stop screaming in the car on the way over, but it was the first time all day. Most everyone had already left, and Jim and I were the only ones in the sanctuary. When I went in and sat down the presence of the Lord was thick.

I sat down and cried. I knew I had sinned, and I knew I could not face the Lord. I figured I would be repenting in my seat for a long time, and I also figured the Lord would be pretty mad at me.

I was wrong. Almost immediately I heard the Lord speak to me. He was not mad at me at all. He said with a little mirth in His voice, "Get up here!"

Obediently I got up and sat down before Him at the communion table, still weak and shaky from being hysterical all day. His grace poured over me and I took communion; forgiven. I didn't have to repent for a long while like I thought I would have to.

His grace has covered our sins. We don't have to cower back in shame. We don't have to worry that we are still not good enough. His grace covers that too.

Grace. We cherish it. We hold in awe and reverence the price Jesus paid for it. And we never take it for granted. But it is not a license to sin.

So, let's get back to our question.

Once saved always saved?

Well, no, but yes!

Chapter Thirteen

The Courts of Heaven

Let us then approach the throne of grace with confidence, so that we may receive mercy and find grace to help us in our time of need. Hebrews 4:16

God does everything on a legal basis. God is not a dictator who just does things on a whim, whatever His divine will is at the moment. He is not like that at all. Everything is done legally with perfect justice. God even obeys His own laws; He is not above the law because He is just and true. There are things that God cannot do, simply because it is against the law. In fact, everything in heaven and earth is run according to His legal system.

Even though Satan is a lawbreaker and will be eternally punished, he knows how to operate in God's legal system. In fact, he knows very well. He has an elaborate case written up against you in that court right now. Satan has access to the courtroom in heaven and he will, until that future day written about in the book of Revelation, when Michael and his angels throw him out.

And war broke out in heaven; Michael and his angels fought with the dragon; and the dragon and his angels fought, but they did not prevail, nor was a place found for them any longer. So, the dragon was cast out, that serpent of old, called the Devil and Satan, who deceives the whole world; he was cast to the earth and his angels were cast out with him. Revelation 12:7-9

Until that day, Satan has judicial rights to appear before the courtroom of heaven. There he makes legal arguments against the saints according to any evidence he may find against us, which when presented gives him a legal access to hinder us. Satan even appears to argue over the souls he feels he has access to after their deaths. He demands his legal rights.

There are many things that can give Satan legal access into your life. The main thing is sin. Your sin or even your ancestor's sin can be brought against you in suit in the heavenly court. Another thing could be the words of your mouth. Satan may gain legal access over you by the things you are speaking. Whether you mean what you are saying or not has no bearing, the actual words that you speak over yourself and your families, words have legal implications. Be careful what you say, because it can and will be used against you.

Have you got prayers and situations that you just can't seem to pray through or get reversed? Chances are there has been a judgement against you by Satan in the courts of heaven that gave him legal access to your life.

This is where the throne of grace comes in and what makes this seat so crucially important to the believers. The throne of grace is a seat that we have obtained legal access to by the blood of Jesus.

At the throne of grace, we can come and receive atonement through repentance that can cancel Satan's lawsuits against us. This is not automatic. If Satan has won a lawsuit against you and obtained a judgement by which he has you held in bondage, then he has a legal right to be there, until you appear before the throne of grace.

At the throne of grace, you may appear and repent for the sin that has been brought against you. You may even repent for others such as your children or ancestors.

The blood of Jesus was a legal transaction that stands in this courtroom. The blood of Jesus through repentance has the power to remove sin. This why we need to appear before the throne of grace, and reverse these lawsuits, and undo what has been done through sin.

Let us therefore come boldly to the throne of grace, that we may obtain mercy and find grace to help in the time of need. Hebrews 4:16

At the throne of grace we can appropriate the legal action that Jesus provided for us when He paid for our sins.

There are a couple very good teachers in the body

of Christ on this subject. They both have teaching on YouTube and books out. One is Robert Henderson and one is Jeanette Strauss.

Jeanette Strauss

Jeanette Strauss learned about the courtroom of heaven and the throne of grace when her daughter, Stacy went through a period of backsliding. Even though Stacy had been raised a Christian she had gotten involved with a non-Christian boyfriend named Mike. She was only seventeen when she got involved with Mike and the relationship went on for years. They tried to talk to Mike about the Lord, but he was not interested. After several years, Stacy even moved out of her parents' house and moved in with Mike and started living his lifestyle. Of course, Jeanette and her husband prayed for Stacy and talked to Stacy, and nothing seemed to be working. The situation only got worse.

One night before bed Jeanette prayed again and asked the Lord how to pray for Stacy. That night she has a dream about the situation. In the dream she faced the strongman that had her daughter bound and he tied her hands. As she was waking up the Lord spoke to her. He said, "**I am the Righteous Judge of heaven and earth. And**

your daughter is a lawful captive of the enemy. Come into my courtroom in heaven; stand in the gap on behalf of the sin that she is committing against Me. Repent for that; ask forgiveness and that I wash her with the blood of Jesus. And that I will move her case from the courtroom of judgement to the throne of grace and mercy, where I will remove the veils off the eyes of her understanding, and she will see the truth and walk in truth."

Jeanette woke up and immediately got up and did as the Lord instructed her to do. Then she pictured a throne, and she handed a file with Stacy's name on it to the Lord who was sitting on it. And she knew something changed.

Seven days later her daughter came running into the house. She had all her belongings in her car. She was moving back home. She told her mother God showed her that Mike was moving her away from God and getting her nowhere. Once her eyes were opened, she packed her bags and immediately got out of there.

When Mike came home from work and found her gone, he began calling her. He told her they could get married, and he would go to church. Mike tried everything, but Stacy would not budge. She was through, after seven years of going nowhere with him.

Stacy eventually married a committed Christian and is raising a family and is still on fire for the Lord.

This story absolutely amazes me. The complete, total, lasting change in Stacy amazes me. The fact that Mike could not sway her amazes me. Stacy saw the seriousness of her situation and she immediately got out. Jeanette has since written a very good book called, *From   the Courtroom of Heaven to the Throne of Grace and Mercy.*

All of Jeanette's prayers had not worked for Stacy because Stacy was a legal captive of the enemy. Satan is the accuser. He knows how to work the legal system. We need to face him in God's courtroom with the blood of Jesus, in a legal way. Otherwise, we are spinning our wheels.

The Real Courtroom

In the spirit realm, which is the real world, there is a legal system in which God is the judge. I know how terrifying standing before a judge in a courtroom can be, I have plenty of experience.

This courtroom is real, and its judgements will affect you for eternity. This is where and when grace becomes the most important thing in the world to you. It is priceless.

And if you have received the gift of the grace of God, your day in court will be a joyful one. {Believe me you do not want to show up in that courtroom without grace!}

Chapter Fourteen

Without Grace

"Therefore, take heed how you hear. For whoever has more will be given; and whoever does not have, even what he seems to have will be taken from him." Luke 8:18

It is all or nothing. With grace we have it all, without grace we have nothing. Without grace even what we think we have, we don't. We will literally be naked in all our sin with nowhere to hide.

Our short little life on earth is our grace period. It is our period to accept grace. Actually, it is even shorter than that. The Bible says, *Behold, now is the accepted time; behold, now is the day of salvation. 2 Corinthians 6:2b.*

We only have now because we don't really know when our life will end. It may be in 5 minutes, or it may be in 50 years. That is why it says now.

I have heard the saying, "Heaven is more wonderful than you can possibly imagine, and hell is more awful than you can possibly imagine." The reality of these words is hard to convey. We are all perched over an eternal destiny in hell, our only hope is God's grace and without grace there is no hope.

When we receive the gift of grace, it comes with an inheritance. Oh, the benefits that come with grace! They are beyond imagination. We receive all the goodness of God. We have His favor. Our name is recorded in the Book of Life. We have purpose and destiny. We become a citizen of heaven, even though we haven't seen it yet, we get an address there. There is a place there being prepared for you. We become part of a huge family. To be in the very lowest place in heaven is better than anything we can imagine on earth. That is only a tiny little sample of the inheritance that comes with grace.

To miss grace is to miss all this. It is to miss everything that God has prepared for you in His great love. The loss is too great for words. But Jesus also said even what you think you have will be taken from you. What does this mean?

Everything good comes from God. Your life, your body, your family and all you love and even the ability to love, all this comes from God. To miss grace means separation from God. This means all that is good will be lost to you and all that remains is evil. Even to those who enjoy evil, believe me, evil without good is way too much evil.

Remember Howard Storm, from the beginning of the book. This man hated God and religion and was not a nice person. But when he found himself in a place with others like himself, who had not a shred of kindness, he was horrified. Suddenly he clung to any trace of good he could remember. Thank goodness Howard received another chance, for without grace he had no hope.

God is only good, so we have to stop blaming Him for evil.

I once met a Jewish lady whom I liked very much. One day the subject came up about God. She said, "God, I don't believe in God!"

I said, "You don't believe in God? But you're Jewish, you must believe in God."

She answered, "Where was God during the holocaust? If there is a God, why did He let my family die?"

"Oh, you do believe in God." I said to her. "You are just angry at Him."

My friend was trying to punish God by saying she did not believe in Him. She was blaming God for evil.

We cannot blame God for evil. God does not do evil.

And don't think but God is God and He controls everything, and He let the evil happen. That is pure ignorance.

Remember God is not lawless, if He was, He would be as bad as Satan and then we really would be hopeless. The end of Hitler's evil came because the righteous on this earth prayed. And also, his end came because the righteous on this earth fought against him and many died.

If you have refused the grace of God because you are blaming God for evil, you are in error. Evil does not come from God, only good.

There is no good reason to refuse grace. It leads to total loss. Those who refuse grace lose everything, absolutely everything. The loss is too great for words. They become truly alone without family, love or any kind of kindness, because everything good comes from God. Without God there is nothing good.

In fact, evil was created at the fall of Satan. The dark world of antimatter came in at that time. The opposite of good came.

Have you ever watched the news after a horrific event such as a fire or tornado or a flood? They show the survivors who are standing in the rubble of what was once their homes and all their possessions. So often they are standing there with such devastation on their faces and tears, and they keep saying, "We've lost everything."

In actuality they only lost their earthly possessions, that loss in very small in comparison to an eternal loss of your soul.

Right now, grace is available. Right now, is the day of salvation. Grace is the golden ticket; with it you have everything. Without it even what you think you have will be taken away.

Please don't let yourself be found without grace!

Chapter Fifteen

The Power of the Age to Come

The age to come is a mystery that we have only begun to peek into. In the age to come those who have become overcomers in this life will rule and reign with Christ. They will have proved themselves worthy to be true sons of God. They will carry His majesty and use His authority. They will sit on thrones with Him. But they will have powers and abilities that seem fantastic in our world.

Throughout history those who have walked in great grace on this earth have tasted the power of the age to come. We will look at some examples of this in the marvelous book of Acts.

*Now Stephen a man full of God's **grace** and power, did great wonders and miraculous signs among the people. Opposition arose, however, from members of the Synagogue of Freedom {as it was called] - Jews of Cyrene and Alexandria as well as the provinces of Cilicia and Asia.*

These men began to argue with Stephen, but they could not stand up against his wisdom or the Spirit by whom he spoke.

Then they secretly persuaded some men to say, "We have heard Stephen speak words of blasphemy against Moses and against God."

So, they stirred up the people and elders and teachers of the law. They seized Stephen and brought him before the Sanhedrin. They produced false witnesses, who testified, "This fellow never stops speaking against this holy place and against the law. For we have heard him say that Jesus of Nazareth will destroy this place and change the customs that Moses handed down to us."

All who were sitting in the Sanhedrin looked intently at Stephen, and they saw that his face was like the face of an angel. Acts 6:6-15NIV

{At this point Stephen gives a long speech, I will skip that part.}

When they heard this, they were furious and gnashed their teeth at him. But Stephen, full of the Holy Spirit looked up to heaven and saw the glory of God and Jesus standing at the right hand of God. "Look" he said, "I see heaven open and the Son of man standing at the right hand of God."

At this they covered their ears and yelling at the top of their voices they all rushed at him, dragged him out of the city and began to stone him. Meanwhile the witnesses laid their clothes at the feet of a young man named Saul.

While they were stoning him, Stephen prayed, "Lord Jesus, receive my spirit." Then he fell on his knees

and cried out, "Lord, do not hold this sin against them."
When he had said this, he fell asleep. Acts 7:54-59NIV

Signs and Wonders

Stephen is a man full of grace and power. We see him in this passage experiencing the powers of the age to come. Let's look at some of these. Stephen, like Jesus, is doing signs and wonders. Some of the signs and wonders Jesus did were healing the sick, casting out demons, raising the dead and even stopping storms. Stephen has grown in grace, and he operates in miracles. These are powers from the age to come. This is supernatural.

Supernatural Wisdom

Stephen has supernatural wisdom. This is also like Jesus; Stephen's enemies are unable to argue with him because he has a wisdom that is beyond this world's wisdom. Stephen frustrates all their arguments so that their only recourse is to lie.

I had something sort of like this happen to me, one time, many years ago when I first became a Christian. I belonged to a denominational church that did not believe in anything supernatural whatsoever. During this time, I read a book by Frances Hunter about speaking in tongues. I did not have the same hang-ups my church did. Reading about this experience thrilled me and I wanted it. I just did not know how to go about it.

I was fourteen at the time and after I read the book I went to a meeting for teens. I told the young people in the meeting about tongues, thinking everyone would be as excited about it as I was. Two much older boys immediately wanted to debate and prove to me this experience was false. I had been a Christian only about six months and had no way to debate them I barely knew any scriptures.

As they tried to disprove to me the truths of the Baptism of the Holy Spirit that I had only recently read about, I tried my best to defend it. I did not know what to tell them, so I opened my Bible. I just happened to open my Bible to a scripture about speaking in tongues. Amazed at the answer right in front of me, I read them the scripture. These guys were ready for me and came at me with more arguments, yet every time they did, I would open my Bible and again the correct scripture would be right there as I needed. This went on for a half hour or more. You would have thought I was Bible scholar. I knew something supernatural was happening and it continued until the boys finally gave up.

They wanted to study and debate with me again at another time, when they were more ready for me. But I couldn't because I didn't even know the scriptures, I was reading them I was just opening to them and reading. It was a supernatural event. It was another six months after that before I visited a full gospel church and spoke in tongues for myself. But I knew it was special because I had received a miracle just talking about it. I frustrated older and wiser Christians that tried to convince me this was not of God, with wisdom that was not my own.

Supernatural wisdom is one of the powers of the age to come.

Transfiguration

Stephen's appearance also changes. His face appears as an angel's face. He begins to shine. His appearance is full of glory. We know Moses had a shining face when he spent time with God on the mountain. Jesus transfigured before Peter James and John, on the Mount of Transfiguration. I believe this is from the age to come. We will be glorious and shine like angels do. Our appearance will reflect the change inside of us; we will reflect the image of Christ.

Seeing into Heaven

Also Stephen is able to see into the heavenly realms from earth. He can look into heaven, and he sees the throne of God and Jesus standing next to Him.

This is supernatural but this has become common.

The internet is swamped with books on people visiting heaven and some on a regular basis. {I am jealous! How cool!} But this is a grace poured out that we can walk in. I believe that especially as the times to come get darker we will walk in greater grace to visit and see into heaven, firstly because we belong there and it is our headquarters, and secondly because we will be working together as one. We will work together with the saints and angels. They haven't forgotten about us; they are intently with us and ready to join with us.

Translocation

We have talked about miracles signs and wonders, supernatural wisdom, seeing into heaven, but there is more. There is translocation, which is traveling instantly to another location which could even be around the globe.

When they came up out of the water, the Spirit of the Lord suddenly took Phillip away, and the eunuch did not see him again, but went on his way rejoicing. Phillip however, appeared at Azotus and traveled about, preaching the gospel in all the towns until he reached Caesarea. Acts8:39-40

Now this topic totally blows my mind. It is like something out of a science fiction movie. But this is beginning to happen more frequently in the body of Christ. The key here is that it is at the Holy Spirit's control. Like Phillip the Holy Spirit is catching believers away to other places to be used by Him.

John Paul Jackson tells a beautiful testimony in a YouTube video about translocation. John Paul was doing a series of conferences in the United Kingdom and the western world. As he left for the conferences he was not feeling well and thought he might be coming down with a cold. As he continued through his itinerary doing conferences, he began to get worse. He prayed for healing, but he continued to go downhill physically until he arrived in Bern, Switzerland. He says he was alone in his hotel room, and he knew he was seriously ill. His body was swollen to the point he could hardly recognize his own facial features, he had turned yellow, and he had terrible pain throughout his abdomen.

Even though he was the only speaker for the conference the next day he told the Lord, "Unless you heal me, I am going to the hospital in the morning."

He was laying there doing what he called "complaining prayer", when he noticed a man standing next to him in his room. The man was very small; he thought under five feet tall. He was very old with dark skin and very weathered looking. John Paul at first thought he was hallucinating. Then it occurred to him that maybe he was an angel. The old man spoke to John Paul and said, "I have come to pray for you that you may be healed."

With that the old man laid his hands on John Paul's abdomen and began to pray. John Paul describes the feeling of warm liquid coming from the man's hands and rolling across his body. As the feeling spread the pain left and he was totally healed. Then as John Paul was looking at the little old man he totally disappeared. Then he was sure he had been an angel sent by God. He began to pray and thank God for sending an angel to him, to heal him.

"I didn't send an angel," John Paul heard God audibly speak to him. This filled John Paul with utter despair, now he thought the devil had healed and he was doomed. The Lord spoke again, "It wasn't him."

"Well, if it wasn't angel and it wasn't the devil who was it? "John Paul asked.

At this point John Paul tells how God took him in a vision to a small village where he sees a hut with a dirt floor. In the hut he sees the man who had just prayed for him, and he is kneeling in prayer. He is crying out to God to be used by Him. He tells God, "I have never been used by You. Is it too late? Am I too old?"

This is when God used this man to pray for John Paul. He translated him from his tiny village hut to the motel room in Bern Switzerland to pray for John Paul.

Then after God showed John Paul this, He told him, "Much of what you do in your ministry from this point on in your life will also be credited to his account in heaven."

This story amazes me! But John Paul isn't the only one who tells of such things. Many Christians are describing similar things. Michael Van Vlymen in his book, *Angelic Visitations and Supernatural Encounters,* tells how he frequently experiences this. Once he was transported to a hospital in another country where he prayed for a room full of children in the children's ward. Another time he went to an African village where he prayed for a young girl and then preached to them a sermon. Though he seemed to be speaking in English it came out in their language. Another time he appeared and gave money to a minister. Michael is used often in this way. This is becoming more common. This is another example of the powers of the age to come.

Seeing into the Future, and Time Travel

God is outside of time. He is present in the past present and future simultaneously. In the powers of the age to come we will be outside of time. The apostle John saw far into the future when he wrote the book of Revelation. What he saw we will experience in our day and age. He went outside of time. Enoch also, the seventh from Adam prophesied of things still to come. Natural man is locked inside of time; those who experience the power of the age to come may transcend time.

I want to talk about John Paul Jackson again. {The first time I heard this I was awestruck. I thought this stuff only happened in Sci-fi movies!} He had an amazing experience that is recorded on YouTube in the sermon, *Getting to Know the God of Time and Space.* John Paul was literally taken back in time.

It all started while John Paul was on a trip to the Holy land and was lying in bed in his hotel room with his wife by his side. Two angels appeared and said, "The Lord has need of you."

And John was sucked up. He knew he was in his body because he saw his wife lying in bed sleeping and he was gone. And much to his amazement, he landed on a street in Jerusalem 3,500 years earlier!

John found himself in an ancient marketplace. He also found he was dressed as the people in that day were. The first thing that happened to him was he started choking. The stench was terrible. The street was filled with vendors selling fish and chickens and melons and many other things, but the smells were horrible. There was dung and urine in the street and the children looked dirty with smudged faces.

He could no longer see the two angels but somehow, he had instructions. He knew what he was supposed to do, and he knew he was not to deviate from his instructions. He was to go up one side of the street and tell the people that David was to be the next king. At this point Saul was still king but David had been anointed to be king.   John Paul began his assignment. He found that he still thought in English, but his words came out in their language, and when the people spoke, he could understand. He began walking up the street telling the people as he was instructed. He stated emphatically this was real, it wasn't a dream.

John Paul got various responses from the people he spoke to. Some people couldn't have cared less who was king. Some agreed with him, and others declared, "David is only a boy, Saul is strong!"

As John was traveling through the crowds telling people about David, someone said to him, "Look there he is, now." John looked and saw David on the other side of the street. It was a narrow street about three chariots wide. David was talking to someone else, but he also was keeping an eye on John, as he continued down the street fulfilling his mission.

John Paul was also having troubled thoughts as he was going along, "How will I get back! I didn't get myself here I don't know how I will get back!" He also worried about his wife and what she would do when she found him missing. He was there for many hours, until he reached the end of the marketplace.

Finally, as John reached the end of his side of the street, he stopped and looked up and he and David's eyes met. David called to him to come to him. As John walked toward him, they met in the middle of the street. David took John's hand in his and it surprised John how small his hand was. David was a small man with dark red hair and blue green eyes.

David looked intently at John and said, "I know who you are, I know where you came from, and we will meet again."

Suddenly a cart came from one direction and donkey from another and John stepped back to let them pass, and then to his surprise John was brought back. He was back in his hotel room next to his wife and no time had passed!

Shaken up and breathless, John Paul asked God, "Why did you do that?"

God answered him. "Son, there is more to the cloud of witnesses than you understand, and I never do anything without a witness."

This is mind bending stuff! I know it was terrifying to John Paul at the time, but I think it is thrilling. God can pull someone out of time and plug them somewhere else and then plug them right back in again. I have trouble bending my mind around this kind of stuff. If he went back into time, did it happen again or was that the only time it happened? If that was the only time it happened, then someone was there who had never even been born yet! How does this work???

I watched all three of the *Back to the Future,* movies, not because I liked the stories so much but because the concept of time travel intrigues me. Especially in the second movie when Marty, the character who is traveling in time, travels back into the fifties for the second time, and sees himself who had traveled back into the future the first time. If you haven't seen the movies, I know I have you confused! The thing that is intriguing about this is that now there are two Martys. Each from a different time!

Time travel is more of those amazing powers of the age to come. John Paul went backward in time I want to mention a man who went forward in time and encountered himself.

Christopher Paul Carter in his book, *In the Palaces of Heaven,* describes just such a thing. Christopher, who frequently travels to heaven and talks about it in his book, he described a day when God brought him to a beautiful garden. What he didn't know at the time was the garden was in the distant future. It was a beautiful garden, very full of life.

Christopher walked up to a man sitting under a tree in front of a delicate golden easel, drawing plans. He said there was a sense of creation about the drawings as if they would become reality when the man was finished.

Christopher stopped and watched. He was amazed at the man's unhurried contentment. He thought maybe this was some saint; Christopher looked to God to ask Him who this was. The Father sent him back to the man and told him to look at his face. Christopher did and froze, it was his own face. He was looking at himself in the distant future.

Christopher goes on to say later in the chapter that on one occasion he was allowed to receive some encouraging words from his "future me" about his future. Although he doesn't tell us what he told himself.

When I read that I was just downright amazed. I thought if he can do that, I can do that. I wanted to talk to my "future me." I told God if Christopher could do it then I could do it. Well, I did not get a trip to heaven or see a beautiful garden, like Christopher did. I would have loved to, but I am not on his level. I did not even hear my own future voice I heard the Holy Spirit's voice, but I did have a conversation with my "future me." What she told me really hit the nail on the head for me.

She told me, "You think that everything will always be the same that nothing will ever change. But," she told me, "That is not true."

I know that of course, but I really don't know it. I have to be honest I have not really enjoyed my life. It has been too heavy and too hard. My biggest struggles are fear and worry. I feel like a little ant trying to carry around a brick. I am looking forward to living in heaven someday, but it seems more like a fairy tale, because my reality is struggle. I can't say I am unhappy though, because I love many things about my life, the Lord, my husband, my children and grandchildren. But we all have such problems.

What she was saying hit home. The real truth is this is only a short time. Things will change. I will be fulfilled, and struggles will cease, and then it will then seem like, "Why did I think that was so hard?"

And then she told to me, "Enjoy every minute of your life, even the bad ones."

This hit home again, I was not letting myself enjoy my life, I have been holding my breath and trying to do my best until it is over. But enjoy the bad moments?! I hardly enjoy the good ones! I have been trying to do this. I have been trying to take her advice. I have been trying to enjoy each moment; I have been trying to remember that soon the struggles will be over.

Animals and Nature Working with Us

Some more of the powers of the age to come have to do with nature and animals. There have been some unusual occurrences with animals in the Bible. The most unusual was when a donkey spoke to Balaam in the book of numbers chapter 22. Balaam's donkey refused to move forward because an angel was in the road with a drawn sword, which Balaam could not see. Balaam was beating the donkey when the donkey spoke to him and asked him why he was beating him. Then the angel appeared and rebuked Balaam.

And then there were the ravens that fed Elijah. The ravens fed Elijah bread and meat in the morning and bread and meat in the evening.

In the age to come we will have a different relationship with the animals. We will be able to communicate with them. St. Frances of Assisi, who lived from the years 1182-1226, had a supernatural relationship with animals. He could communicate with animals, and he felt at one with nature.

He would preach to the birds, and they did not fear him. He was most famous for taming a killer wolf that was terrorizing the town of Gubbio. So vicious was this wolf it had not only killed animals, but people as well. Those who went after were attacked. The townspeople were so afraid they dare not leave the city walls.

Francis went out after the wolf even though the townspeople tried to stop him. When the wolf came charging at him out of the woods with teeth barred, Francis made the sign of the cross and the power of God came on the wolf and slowed him down and the wolf's mouth shut. Then the Saint called out to the wolf, "Come to me Brother Wolf, In the name of Christ I order you not to hurt anyone." At that the wolf came and lay down at St Francis' feet. Then he told the wolf, "Brother Wolf I want to make peace between you and the people of Gubbio. They will not hurt you anymore and you must not hurt them. All past crimes will be forgiven."

Then Francis held out his hand and the wolf placed his paw in his hand. The wolf meekly followed St. Frances to the town and Frances made a pact with the wolf and the people. They were to feed him, and he was to never harm them in any way. Again, the wolf received the pact by placing his paw in the Saints hand. From that time on the pact was kept. The wolf lived among the townspeople going from door to door for food. Even the dogs would not bark at him. The wolf lived for two more years and then died of old age, and he was missed by the townspeople.

St Francis was operating in the powers of the age to come with the animals. We've had little peeks, from scripture of that time, such as of wolves lying down with lambs. {Isaiah 11:6}

My daughter Joy is one who really loves animals. My daughter has three small children who are very close in age and are quite a handful. Any animal she gets has to be quite durable with three children loving squeezing and playing with it.

Mr. Cuddles was one such an animal. He was their cat, a tough yellow and white tomcat. When Joy went to the shelter to find a cat, Mr. Cuddles found them. He warmed up to all of them immediately. Mr. Cuddles was like an angel. He seemed to help Joy with the kids. Joy has a special needs child who would yell and scream. Mr. Cuddles took it on himself to help. He would sleep with whatever child needed him the most. He also kept their house clear of the constant stream of mice that would try to move in from the field behind their house, even though it sometimes made him sick. When Joy added a Chihuahua, named Ellie, to the family Mr. Cuddles warmed up to her too. Joy depended on Mr. Cuddles, and he was there for her.

After several years of Mr. Cuddles caring for Joy and her family, one day Mr. Cuddles was nowhere to be found. Everyone in the family searched for him. Little Ellie the Chihuahua finally found him in the field behind the house. Even in death Mr. Cuddles was thinking of his family, he went out to the field to die. The family mourned Mr. Cuddles.

Several weeks ago, Joy came over and told me Mr. Cuddles had visited her from heaven. She went out in the backyard early in the morning, and in the spirit, Mr. Cuddles came to her. She saw him. She said he only stayed for a minute. He had something he wanted to tell her. He told her he was sorry for leaving her, but he was very sick. That was all he wanted to say, that he was sorry he had to go. He loved his family, and he took their care very seriously.

In the powers of the age to come we will communicate with animals.

Back to Stephen

The Bible tells us Stephen was a man of grace and power. We see that he can be trusted with this power. He is very Christ like. Stephen has acquired such a measure of God's grace that he has begun operating in the powers of the age to come. He has supernatural power. Stephen does not use this supernatural power to save his life; instead, he uses this power to lay down his life for his Savior, Jesus.

Stephen has grown in grace and the results are obvious. He has literally become like Jesus. He walks in the same manner of humility and sacrifice, wisdom and power.

The last thing Stephen does on earth is the same thing Jesus also did from the cross. Stephen prays for those who are brutally murdering him. He asks God to forgive them.

Stephen has been transformed into the image of Christ. He has obtained a great measure of grace and he has fulfilled his purpose in this life. He has entered eternity in honor and his rewards are endless.

Those who have walked in this way, through the ages, have fixed their focus on the eternal realm. They are not living for the temporary rewards of earth.

So, we fix our eyes not on what is seen, but on what is unseen. For what is seen is temporary but what is unseen is eternal.2 Corinthians 4:18 NIV

Those in the past generations, like Stephen and those to come in our generation who focus their lives on the eternal, and who grow in grace, who become like Christ, they will also walk in the powers of the age to come. But like Christ, these powers will be used to fulfill God's purpose in their lives and to love God and others.

Conclusion

Chapter Sixteen

So, Just What is Grace?

So just what is grace?

To completely understand grace, we have to be aware of the huge mess that we are in. Without dramatic help we are all set up for an eternity without God.

One of our biggest hindrances to knowing our true spiritual condition is pride.

We do not want to admit we are sinners, so we compare ourselves to someone worse than we are and that is our meter for righteousness. The problem is it doesn't work, because the true meter for righteousness is God's righteousness.

God's righteousness is so overwhelmingly pure that it causes us to want to hide.

I had an experience one time, where I became

aware of God and His holiness, and I literally thought I was going to die. This was after I had been a Christian for many years, and I was pretty much a goody two shoes.

But next to God's holiness I felt wretched. I realized how selfish my thoughts and actions were. My speech even though it is pretty clean by human standards, was causing me great discomfort and seemed filthy, my thoughts as well.

God is literally pure. Next to His holiness, in my human condition, I was filthy. I was undone! I realized we are hopeless without grace! Only the work of grace will make us truly holy.

We are ready for grace when we see our true condition.

Seeing Our True Condition

In chapter one, we talked about Howard Storm, a man who hated God, religion and everything about both. He was a prideful selfish and angry man. He was the last person that anyone would ever dream of becoming a minister! Yet he left his career he was so proud of and became a minister. What happened in between?

He died and his spirit left his body. In that state he came face to face with his true spiritual condition. His horror was beyond words. Seeing his true condition and facing eternity in this condition made grace precious to him.

Obviously, he was given another chance and he is

still alive today. But now he lives to tell others of grace.

When I look back at the time in my life when I came to the Lord at fourteen years old, I see grace at work in my life. God orchestrated a careful plan to bring me to Him. He started tearing down all the things that I was holding onto, in the process, opening my eyes to the true spiritual reality and the condition of my soul.

I saw that I meant nothing to the rebellious crowd I was a part of.

I saw that the things that I had done were not cool but horrible and I was terribly ashamed.

I saw that I had mistreated the people that really cared about me to the point they were fed up with me.

I saw that I was a prisoner of darkness and darkness was repulsive.

I hated myself, my life and everything about me. I was miserable. I was finally ready for grace.

My twin sister, Carol had gotten saved a few months before me and she was praying for me. She had tried to tell me about Jesus, but it enraged me. She continued to pray. This is when God opened my eyes to my true spiritual condition.

When I look at the events that led up to my salvation, I feel fear and awe. I was totally sold out to darkness. How did Jesus manage to rescue me? I was so close to hell and the devil had me in his grip.

Grace's first work in me was to have my life and every relationship fall apart. My life became so dark, actually it had been all along but now I could see it. My sister and her constant talk about Jesus were no longer

repulsive to me, it became my only light. I started following her around. I even slept on her bedroom floor. And that is where I was, on her bedroom floor.
I was laying there crying. I had been crying for days. She was on her bed talking about how Jesus loved me, I had heard it before. But this time, as she was talking, Jesus walked through her door and stood over me on the floor. He told me for Himself that He loved me.

He reached out to me, and I reached back.

That was forty-one years ago. Forty-one years ago, this door called grace opened to me and I stepped in. Now I live in grace. I never want to leave grace. It is such a wonderful place. It is a place in my heart, a secret place that has kept me through the years. Jesus loves....**me.** He has saved....**me.** He died on the cross for...**me.** He is with....**me.**

What is grace? It was my last hope, and it was my only hope.

More about Grace

The word grace is used so widely and so often in the Bible that its meaning becomes manifold.

Grace:
Caused Jesus to die on the cross for us
Gives us right standing before God and allows us to stand clean before Him
Grace covers us until we are transformed into His

image

      Grace is poured out upon us.

      Grace multiplies.

      We are to use it in our speech.

      We are to use it in our actions.

      It rests upon the humble and lifts him up.

      It gives the weak, the greatest strength.

      It helps us through our sufferings.

      It contains incomparable riches.

      It has the power to heal, deliver and raise from the dead.

      It was given to us before the beginning of time.

      It is frequently used with the words mercy, peace and love.

      It is abundant.

      We are to continue in it.

      Nothing can penetrate it because it is the safest place to be.

      It saves from an eternity in hell.

      It is our hope, without it we have no hope.

      It is God's unmerited favor.

      It was costly.

      It is holy.

      .It is eternal

A Life of Grace

      When God saved me, He did not just get me and

put me on a shelf and keep me there waiting for heaven. That was my plan but that was not His plan.

You see, even though I was saved now I did not want to put forth any effort in to living. I did not like living too much, so I just wanted life to be over already. I did not want to try. I had no plans or ambition. I had no feelings or emotions, it kept me from pain. I had myself wrapped up in a shell, and I wasn't coming out. I was thankful for my salvation, but I wasn't willing to live. Pressing into God wasn't a big issue because I was motionless. I thought maybe I could be a martyr in a foreign country and just skip to the heaven part. God had a real problem with me, His work had just begun.

God's grace wasn't over. As carefully as God had orchestrated my salvation, was as carefully as He has orchestrated my entire life.

God interrupted my inertia when He brought my husband, Jim into my life. All of a sudden, I wanted something! I wanted something with all my being. I wanted to be married to Jim and have a life. The problem was that the something I wanted was completely impossible. Jim was too big of a mess, and I was too big of a mess.

Life changed for me immediately once Jim was in my life. I had trouble, trouble, trouble. If I wanted Jim, then I wanted trouble. The choice was there of course, emptiness or trouble. God has since showed me He was very pleased with my choice. I chose love, even though love meant pain. I chose the way of suffering, I chose to suffer for the love of someone else, Jim, but it was life for me, not death. It got me living. This was my higher calling. {Although no one would believe this. I have been told so many times I married out of God's will I lost count, mostly by ministers.}

Now I had to put forth effort. I had to pray without ceasing. I had to fight, I had to claw my way and trudge endlessly for years on end. I had to hurt and feel pain and learn how to forgive and forgive and forgive and forgive. [It is not easy living with an alcoholic.}

I had chosen a hard and heavy path, an impossible path, a path I could not do alone. I took the path that required grace, greater grace. I could not find my own way on this path; it took complete obedience to God. I was helpless on my own. If God told me to go this way, I had to go that way I had to, I had no choice. Many times, God told me to do things I did not want to do, I thought I could not, they were too difficult. But I had to, I had to follow Him, I could not handle this path alone.

I had to stay with Jim when I wanted to leave.

Leave Jim when I wanted to stay.

3 times we left everything and moved.

I have had to face, policemen and judges, lawyers and probation officers, people I would rather hide from.

I have known poverty, turmoil, frustration, rage, hopelessness, and fear.

I have had wondered how my kids would turn out in all this turmoil.

I have had to fast, pray all night, pray all day, believe God for the impossible.

I have cried many tears, wailed, hollered and

screamed.

Does this really sound like the path that God has chosen for me? Does God choose suffering for people? Does any good come from suffering? Is this grace?

Yes, yes, yes and yes. First of all, my suffering is not meaningless. Not in my life, in Jim's life or in our children's life. What looks like total loss from our world's perspective is often times gain in an eternal perspective and from God's point of view.

When Jesus suffered everyone thought His cause was lost. They did not understand the true gain that was made from His suffering. They wanted Him to be king and overthrow the Roman government. Instead, He was killed like a common criminal. They misunderstood the plan of God which was much higher and more important than the end of their immediate problem of the Romans and Israel. This was the price of grace, and this was the most important event ever, and His disciples and loved ones thought all was lost. They only saw defeat.

God's plans are not always evident until we get an eternal perspective on things.

God has an eternal purpose in my life and my family's life. Anything we have suffered is very minimal in comparison. Not that I have an understanding of what it is all about now, on this side of eternity. No, I don't. I only have a tiny glimpse, and that hardly seems real. But on this side of eternity, I can tell you I have experienced God's grace. Over and over again I have experienced God's grace. I have lived a life of grace. God made possible the impossible, although it wasn't easy. The difficult path is a good path because it means more grace.

So, What is Grace?

How can I sum up the answer to our question in a clear and simple way?

Let's start with this:

The price of grace was so high that its value is inconceivable. Grace is so holy and so precious it is to be treated with absolute reverence and awe. The riches of grace are incomparable.

Our grace period is now. We have only one chance, salvation through the blood of Jesus. There is no other way to grace, none, and our opportunity for grace is only now. Those who pass from this life without grace will never receive another chance.

Grace covers us so we are right with God. We are being formed into the image of Christ but until that time we are covered by grace.

Grace is eternal.

Grace is undeserved.

Grace is our only hope.

Grace does not mean we will not suffer, but it does mean our suffering will have purpose, eternal purpose.

So, what is grace? Let's start again.

Grace is needed because we, the human race, are a fallen race. When Satan rebelled against God and fell, he deceived one third of the angels to follow him. Satan and the fallen angels are doomed. They have no hope. They will suffer eternal judgement in the Lake of Fire, and they know this.

Jealous, Satan enticed our forefather Adam to disobey God and Adam fell. Our fate was now to join them, Satan and his angels in eternal judgement. We faced the same hopelessness.

Except, God gave His only Son, Jesus, to take our place, when He came to earth in human form and died on the cross.

Now through grace we have a choice. We can choose whom we will serve.

Satan, so jealous of the grace offered to us, still entices mankind to follow him, so he can vent his rage, of his great loss, on those God so loves and offered this grace. He wants you to give up what he can't have. If he can't do that, he wants to take it from you another way.

He wants to convince you to sin willfully and trample your priceless gift under foot.

Grace is not automatic we have to come to God in repentance and receive His grace. Grace is the answer to our one big problem, but in answering that one problem it answers our every problem.

Grace is invisible. It is not something we can see and hold in our hands. And yet it is the most valuable thing in the universe. So valuable there is an invisible war going on over you. It started with Adam, but it is still going on over you personally.

First there was a great spiritual war to give you grace. That war could only be won by Jesus and that war was won by great suffering and humility. Now there is a war over your personal soul, to keep you from grace. Again humility is a key.

Satan does not want you to know the true value of grace.

Actually, your human mind cannot comprehend the true value of grace. You have eons to discover it. Your job now is just to receive it. Then cherish it and hold it in awe.

Grace is our answer.

So, what is grace?

In its simplest form, grace is the love of God expressed toward us in the sacrifice of His Son Jesus.

With grace we have everything, without grace even what we think we have will be taken away.

So, grace is the ticket to everything good.

So, what is grace?
In Summer's language..... grace is the ticket, the golden ticket!

Epilogue

This ending is for anyone that may have somehow picked up this book and you have never given your life to Jesus. His grace, His wonderful grace is being offered to you right now. It is priceless. With it your sins will be forgiven, and you will have right standing with God. This is the reason Jesus came to this earth and suffered, in your place. A great price was paid to give you this grace. Will you receive it? It is your only hope. Pray with me.

Jesus, please forgive me for my sins and come into my heart. I receive your grace. I receive your love. I want to live for you. Cover me with your grace. Amen

A new door has just opened. It is the door of grace. You are perfect in God's sight; you are welcome here in His presence. You belong here now. You are home.

Notes

Introduction…..*The Final Quest*, by Rick Joyner

Morningstar Publications

Page,55

Chapter 1………Howard Storm…www.youtube.com {testimony of Howard Storm}

Chapter3……*The Final Quest*, by Rick Joyner

Morningstar Publications,

Pages,71, 73,84

The Archko Volume, translated by Drs. McIntosh and Twyman

McGraw Hill,

Pages,141-142

Chapter 4…….Its Supernatural, with Sid Roth

sidroth.org, Guest, Shawn Bolz {television show}

Angels on Assignment, by Roland Buck

Chapter 8......*Jesus Freaks,* by dc Talk and the Voice of the Martyrs

Albury publishing, Tulsa Ok

Page,144

Chapter 13......From the Courtroom of heaven to the Throne of Mercy and Grace {sermon}

www.youtube.com

Chapter 15....John Paul Jackson

www.youtube.com

Testimony to Make You Cry

Getting to Know the God of Time and Space {sermon}

www.ingramcontent.com/pod-product-compliance
Lightning Source LLC
LaVergne TN
LVHW011353080426
835511LV00005B/269